Alternative Dispute Resolution in the Regulatory Process

Alternative Dispute Resolution in the Regulatory Process

Deirdre McCarthy Gallagher, Richard Miles, and Jerrilynne Purdy

Michigan State University Press | *East Lansing*

⊗ The paper used in this publication meets the minimum requirements
of ANSI/NISO Z39.48-1992 (R 1997) (Permanence of Paper).

Michigan State University Press
East Lansing, Michigan 48823-5245

LIBRARY OF CONGRESS CATALOGING-IN-PUBLICATION DATA
Names: McCarthy Gallagher, Deirdre, author. | Miles, Richard L., author. | Purdy, Jerrilynne, author.
Title: Alternative dispute resolution in the regulatory process / Deirdre McCarthy Gallagher,
Richard Miles, and Jerrilynne Purdy.
Description: East Lansing : Michigan State University Press, 2020.
Series: Public utility regulation | Includes bibliographical references.
Identifiers: LCCN 2019022091
ISBN 978-1-61186-342-0 (pbk. : alk. paper)
ISBN 978-1-60917-618-1 (pdf)
ISBN 978-1-62895-381-7 (epub)
ISBN 978-1-62896-382-3 (kindle)
Subjects: LCSH: Arbitration (Administrative law)—United States.
| Public utilities—Law and legislation—United States.
Classification: LCC KF5417 .G35 2020 | DDC 347.73/9—dc23
LC record available at https://lccn.loc.gov/2019022091

Book design by Charlie Sharp, Sharp Des!gns, Lansing, MI
Cover design by Erin Kirk New
Cover artwork © Sebastian423 | Dreamstime.com

Michigan State University Press is a member of the Green Press Initiative and is
committed to developing and encouraging ecologically responsible publishing
practices. For more information about the Green Press Initiative and the use of
recycled paper in book publishing, please visit www.greenpressinitiative.org.

Visit Michigan State University Press at *www.msupress.org*

CONTENTS

PREFACE

As energy and environmental issues become more complex, efforts to address these issues become more contentious and prolonged. Multiple stakeholders, highly technical subjects, significant financial implications combine to raise the stakes and heighten the need for alternatives to litigation to wade through the issues. But why does this happen?

Because adversarial litigation may take years, even decades, impacting project implementation and the relationships essential to effect any agreements. The good news is that this reality is well understood by the federal and state agencies profiled in this book, who have made concerted and committed efforts to integrate dispute resolution process alternatives into their work. This does not mean that disputes have disappeared or that litigation is no longer an appropriate option to settle regulatory disputes. There are still disputes, some of which call for the definitive or authoritative resolution of issues through litigation. However, when parties have concerns or complaints, whether filed or not, they have options for where to go within the respective regulatory agency to voice—and hopefully resolve—concerns. Perhaps more importantly, private parties who are equipped to utilize the dispute resolution alternatives profiled in this book have the chance to pursue resolution on their own, prior to agency action. Often, parties that participate in negotiation leading to resolution heighten their chances of an agency accepting a settlement that reflects what is important to them, rather than what an agency might think is best for them.

The path to develop and institutionalize dispute resolution options may be challenging. Introducing new process options is not a simple task, especially when the new options challenge the paradigm for an agency or private organization and for parties accustomed to a win-lose model. Integrating dispute resolution process options requires a culture change, a willingness to recognize that there may be more than one way to solve a problem. As Abraham Maslow once said, "If you only have a hammer, you tend to see every problem as a nail." The culture change from a litigation-focused approach to a settlement or resolution-oriented approach in the regulatory arena that has occurred over the past twenty-five-plus years required developing and making available tools other than hammers to approach problems differently and to carve out different paths toward resolution.

One of the purposes of this book is to reflect on the culture change toward dispute resolution, first in the federal realm through the lens of the Federal Energy Regulatory Commission (FERC or Commission) as it was at the time of writing. The coauthors experienced firsthand the evolution at FERC and, in many instances, contributed to it. Rick Miles was a FERC litigator who later served as the Director of the Office of Administrative Litigation and was the founder and Director of the FERC Dispute Resolution Service (DRS). DRS is an independent unit in FERC that provides alternative dispute resolution (ADR) services to parties for FERC-related matters and is discussed in detail later. Jerrilynne Purdy worked for fourteen years with a major electric utility before bringing her expertise to FERC in different advisory staff positions and later as a dispute resolution specialist and trainer with the DRS. And Deirdre McCarthy Gallagher worked both internationally and domestically as a dispute resolver before joining the FERC DRS team as an attorney-mediator, trainer, and manager. The coauthors participated in the DRS-related cases described in this book (all publicly filed with FERC), as well as in all of the trainings discussed in the training and outreach section. In reflecting on this experience and on lessons learned at FERC, the coauthors are inspired by what has been accomplished.

Equally inspiring is the work of state regulatory agencies, the California Public Utilities Commission, the New York Public Service Commission, and the Michigan Public Service Commission, as evidenced by information reported by the coauthors on program options and impacts. Each of the dispute resolution programs profiled is unique, demonstrating an approach that is not cookie cutter but reflective of the unique needs of the respective agency and its constituency. Each of the agencies showcased here made concerted efforts to tailor its dispute resolution program to its organization and constituency. The dispute resolution programs and the processes offered are different because the needs are different. Their programs are successful insofar as they respond to these needs.

For the coauthors, this book reflects our commitment to and passion for dispute resolution as a powerful alternative to enhance input, creativity, and effectiveness of resolutions in the regulatory arena. We are inspired to tell these stories to showcase what has been achieved and, more importantly, to highlight the possibilities moving forward, whether in expanding the dispute resolution alternatives at these agencies or in fortifying dispute resolution alternatives at other federal and state agencies. In addition, the lessons and guidance shared are easily transferable to regulated entities and companies in the private sector. Ultimately, it is up to the parties to use and embrace dispute resolution. We believe that when agency and business leaders take a more active role in advancing dispute resolution, then the culture shift from a litigation-focused approach to a settlement-oriented approach will sustain itself.

ACKNOWLEDGMENTS

Our foremost thanks to Dr. Janice Beecher, Director of the Michigan State University Institute of Public Utilities, who invited us to write this book and provided input and encouragement throughout the process. Thanks also to those who gave their time, energy, and information, including: Jane Juliano, Chief of the Alternative Dispute Resolution Unit of the United States Office of Special Counsel, who reviewed the draft and offered insight from a seasoned mediator's perspective; Harvey Reiter, partner with Stinson Leonard Street LLP and adjunct professor of Regulated Industries at the George Washington University Law School, who graciously reviewed the draft and provided thoughtful input; and Carmen Cintron, Chief Administrative Law Judge of the Federal Energy Regulatory Commission, who provided insight on the chapter on settlement judges. We also owe a debt of gratitude to the state utility regulators who provided invaluable information about their dispute resolution programs: John E. Thorson, former Assistant Chief Administrative Law Judge, Jean Vieth, former Administrative Law Judge and Alternative Dispute Resolution Program Coordinator, and Kimberly H. Kim, Administrative Law Judge and Alternative Dispute Resolution Program Coordinator, and Phillip Enis, Program Manager, Consumer Protection and Enforcement Division, with the California Public Utilities Commission; Elizabeth Liebschutz, Chief Administrative Law Judge, and Elizabeth Grisaru, Policy Advisor, with the New York Public Service Commission; Susan Corbin, Director of the Customer Assistance Division, and Mike Byrne, Director of the Strategic Operations Division, with the Michigan Public Service Commission; and Sharon Feldman, Administrative Law Judge with the Michigan Administrative Hearing System.

INTRODUCTION

Conflict is natural and inevitable. It happens to everyone. The key is not to avoid it but to manage it effectively. In this book, we explore ways to maximize the opportunity of conflict to promote learning and positive outcomes. We do this through a careful examination of the integration of ADR process options into the federal and state regulatory arenas. We introduce the Voices of Value Model, which provides a roadmap to develop dispute resolution systems. Central to this model is integrating the voices of those impacted by regulatory disputes, essential to ensuring that the dispute resolution system reflects and addresses the needs of those who will use it.

Regulatory agencies have always had the responsibility of adjudicating and decision-making in disputes covering a wide range of subjects. Regulatory agencies rely heavily on traditional processes, such as paper reviews, rulemakings, formal hearings, trials before Administrative Law Judges (ALJs), and appellant reviews, to decide outcomes. In each of these processes, an independent entity, such as an ALJ or a group of commissioners or appellate judges, makes a decision that the parties or agencies are obligated to follow.

As far back as the 1970s, it was recognized that traditional administrative processes did not always meet the needs of the consumers, regulated entities, and regulators. The American Bar Association's Commission on Law and the Economy 1979 report, *Federal Regulation: Roads to Reform,* described the shortcomings of the administrative processes, stating:

> We share the general view that many administrative procedures are too slow, costly and cumbersome. As a result, vital economic interests concerned with capital formation, plant modernization and business expansion are severely handicapped,

and reforms necessary for the protection of workers and consumers are too long postponed. These delays and excessive costs have resulted, in considerable part, from the fact that administrative procedures, initially developed as a safeguard against the threat of regulatory abuse, have come to mimic the judicial process, with inadequate regard for the flexibility available under existing statutes. Improved procedures will serve all citizens, both as consumers and producers.[1]

While some regulatory agencies took steps to shorten their regulatory processes, it could still take months, even years, to achieve final resolution.

This challenge was not unique to the regulatory realm. Chief Justice Warren Burger pointed out in his keynote address at the Pound Conference: Perspectives on Justice in the Future in 1976:

> The topics selected for this conference will inevitably provoke cries that our objective is to reduce access to the courts. Of course, that is not the objective, for what we seek is the most satisfactory, the speediest, and the least expensive means of meeting the legitimate needs of the people in resolving disputes. We must therefore open our minds to consideration of means and forums that have not been tried before.[2]

During the years following Burger's remarks, that is exactly what happened, with legal and business entities exploring creative approaches to settle their disputes. Though the roots of ADR run deep, the concepts began to take root in the early 1980s.[3] The publication of *Getting to Yes* by Robert Fisher and William Ury of the Harvard Negotiation Project in 1981 popularized an alternative approach to negotiating disputes, and the legal profession took notice.

The federal government also took notice. In 1982, the Administrative Conference of the United States (ACUS) initiated a process to address how federal agencies could, and should, use ADR.[4] On June 20, 1986, ACUS adopted Recommendation No. 86-3 with the purpose of promoting "increased, and thoughtful, use of ADR methods." The recommendations went on to say:

> Administrative agencies, where not inconsistent with statutory authority, should adopt the alternative methods discussed in this recommendation for resolving a broad range of issues. These include matters that arise as a part of formal or informal

adjudication, in rulemaking, in issuing or revoking permits, and in settling disputes, including litigation brought by or against the government.[5]

Marshall J. Breger, Chair of ACUS, wrote in 1987:

Given the enormous numbers of adjudications and other disputes that agencies decide, or are parties to, the successful use of ADR in even a small proportion of cases can produce better and fairer decisions, gains in efficiency, savings of time and energy, and ultimately foster greater confidence in government.[6]

Chairman Breger went on to say:

By using more consensual approaches to dispute resolution whenever possible, the federal government can itself become a model for a constructive approach to problem solving.

In fact, the federal government can, and should, take an active leadership role in the ADR area. As party to more controversies than any other entity, the government has a special opportunity to assess the viability of ADR opportunities, use them aptly, and serve as an example for the rest of our society. It must be recognized, however, that the government has unique obligations that may often make use of these alternatives difficult, or even inappropriate.

It is time, therefore, to evaluate ADR's potential for federal agencies and to address directly the social, economic, political and procedural problems that are of concern ... By using more consensual approaches to dispute resolution whenever possible, the federal government can itself become a model for a constructive approach to problem solving.[7]

The seeds of ADR Programs began to spread in the 1990s with Congressional bipartisan support for increased ADR use. Congress passed the Administrative Dispute Resolution Act of 1990 (1990 ADR Act), signed into law by President George Bush on November 15, 1990.[8] The 1990 ADR Act promotes the use of alternative means of dispute resolution within the administrative agencies of the federal government. ADR under the 1990 ADR Act refers to any voluntary procedure used in place of traditional adjudication to resolve matters in controversy, including conciliation, facilitation, mediation, fact finding, and arbitration.[9]

The 1990 ADR Act, which had a sunset provision date of October 1, 1995, was intended to support efforts to develop or enhance ADR Programs with government-wide emphasis on alternative techniques. The 1990 ADR Act:

- Promoted ADR in the federal government;
- Required federal agencies to: develop a policy to address the use of ADR to resolve disputes; designate a senior official to implement the ADR policy and serve as the agency Dispute Resolution Specialist; and provide training in ADR theory and practice to the Dispute Resolution Specialist and other employees involved in ADR;
- Asserted that ADR is a voluntary procedure as an alternative to traditional litigation; and
- Said that ADR may be used only if the parties agree to an ADR proceeding.[10]

Congress extolled the value of the five-year experiment, concluding that the availability of a wide range of dispute resolution procedures and an increased understanding of the most effective use of such procedures would enhance the operation of the government and better serve the public.[11] In 1996, Congress reenacted the 1990 ADR Act without a sunset provision (1996 ADR Act).[12] The ADR seeds planted in the 1980s flourished.

In the federal regulatory arena, recognition of the value of settlement was endorsed well before the 1990 ADR Act. Consider the example of the Federal Energy Regulatory Commission (FERC or the Commission). FERC is an independent federal agency that: regulates the transmission and wholesale sales of electricity and natural gas in interstate commerce; regulates the transportation of oil by pipeline in interstate commerce; reviews proposals to build interstate natural gas pipelines, natural gas storage projects, and liquefied natural gas terminals; and issues licenses for nonfederal hydropower projects. Well before 1990, FERC emphasized

the importance of voluntary settlements to the orderly and expeditious conduct of its business. During the period when responsibility for administering the Natural Gas Act and the Federal Power Act was in the hands of the Federal Power Commission, that agency had a strong policy favoring the disposition of cases through settlements. The FPC and the courts recognized that the Commission could not possibly cope with the flood of business engendered by its jurisdictional statutes if the outcome of a substantial proportion of that business were not the result of voluntary settlements entered into by the parties. *See Mitchell Energy Corp. v. FPC,* 519 F.2d 36, 40 (5th Cir. 1975); *Texas Eastern Transmission Corp. v. FPC,* 306 F.2d 345, 347 (5th Cir. 1962). We [FERC] adhere to that view.[13]

In 1992, Section 1802(e) of the Energy Policy Act of 1992 required FERC, to the maximum extent practicable, to "establish appropriate alternative dispute resolution procedures, including required negotiations and voluntary arbitration, early in an oil pipeline rate proceeding as a method preferable to adjudication in resolving disputes relating to the rate."[14] And in 1994, the Commission reaffirmed its endorsement of settlements, noting:

> It is the policy of the Commission to conclude that ADR can occur at any time during the processing of a filing, whether the filing is subject to informal adjudicatory procedures or to the formal hearing process. The Commission has also noted that participants can pursue ADR methods on their own to resolve potential disputes before an application or other filing is submitted to the Commission.[15]

In its Congressional Performance Budget Request for Fiscal Year 2016, FERC stated:

> The Commission recognizes the value of resolving issues through consensual means where possible. Settling cases benefits energy consumers as it dramatically limits the time, expense, and resources that the Commission and outside parties would otherwise need to devote to these cases. A settlement not only provides ratepayers reduced rates and refunds far more quickly than litigation, but also provides business certainty and facilitates the construction of needed infrastructure in a more timely manner.[16]

Similarly, at the state level, support for dispute resolution processes became more widespread and institutionalized. For example, the state of Washington's administrative code provides that the Washington Utilities and Transportation Commission must include in the procedural schedule for each adjudication the date for an initial settlement conference.[17] In 2005, the California Public Utilities Commission committed to increased ADR use through its resolution "Expanding the Opportunities for and Use of Alternative Dispute Resolution."[18]

In short, at the federal and state levels, regulatory agencies have, over the past thirty years, sought to make their processes more effective, more responsive, and less costly. Out of necessity, many looked to ADR. And although some regulatory agencies have incorporated ADR to resolve regulatory disputes, there is still much to learn and much work to do to institutionalize ADR Programs in the regulatory arena. As budgets tighten amid ever-present demands, the mounting challenge of managing problems efficiently and effectively may move ADR from the realm of "alternative" to the realm of "necessary."

PART 1

Situating Alternative Dispute Resolution in the Regulatory Environment

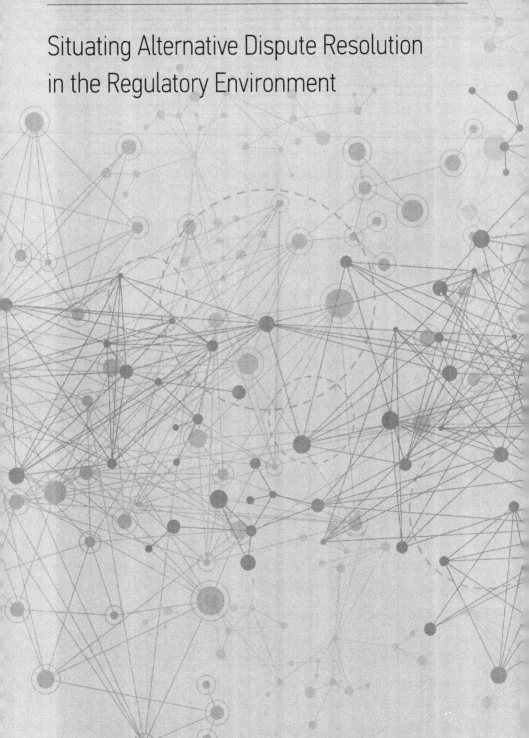

CHAPTER 1

Coming Together of the Regulatory Context and ADR Tools

In the introduction, we observed that traditional approaches to resolving regulatory disputes may not always meet the needs of the regulatory stakeholders. In other words, the opportunity of alternative conflict resolution approaches is often missed. Two things are needed in order to understand the reasons for this: first, a look at the regulatory context, from the origin of regulatory agencies to the traditional processes that developed in this realm; and second, a look at the nature of conflict and ADR process options. With this information in hand, we will be equipped to better answer the question: how can ADR address disputes involving participants in the federal and state regulatory arenas?

Regulatory Context

Over the last two centuries, the perspective of the federal government has evolved from a "laissez-faire" approach to a more active regulatory role that promotes competition, free enterprise, health, safety, and protection of the public interest. This evolution reflects the continual tension between the different perspectives. As Martin Shapiro stated, "In short, regulatory statutes represent an uneasy compromise between laissez faire and government-control visions of the economy."[1]

The utility arena was a focal point of this shift, with public utility regulation first appearing at the state level in the late 1800s and early 1900s through municipal franchises. States began to pass laws authorizing municipal governments to directly regulate the rates charged by gas and electric companies, as well as other utilities. In 1887, Massachusetts was the first state to create a commission to regulate public utilities. Other states (e.g., Georgia, New York, and Wisconsin in 1907; Vermont in 1908; and Michigan in 1909) soon followed, establishing state regulatory commissions.

External support was influential in the proliferation of regulation, with the National Civic Federation reporting in 1907: "Public utilities are so constituted that it is impossible for them to be regulated by competition. Therefore, they must be controlled and regulated by the government; or they must be left to do as they please; or they must be operated by the public. There is no other course. None of us are in favor of leaving them to their own will."[2] The years between 1910 and 1920 witnessed rapid growth, with twenty-nine other states establishing state public utility commissions.[3]

The creation of the first regulatory agencies brought with it challenges to the agencies' decision-making processes. In 1938, Roscoe Pound, chairman of a special committee of the American Bar Association on administrative law, "excoriated the regulatory system for 'administrative absolutism' and catalogued the suspect 'tendencies' of administrative agencies," among them to decide without a hearing, on the basis of matters not before the tribunal, and on the basis of preformed opinions; disregard jurisdictional limits; do what they will to get by; and mix up rulemaking, investigation, and prosecution, as well as the functions of advocate, judge, and enforcement authority.[4]

In 1939, President Roosevelt directed his attorney general to examine what was needed to reform the field of administrative law. The resulting report served as the foundation for Congress' passage of the Administrative Procedure Act of 1946 (APA),[5] in which Congress recognized the role of settlements in the administrative process. APA Section 554(c)(1) highlights the inclusion of parties in this process, providing:

> The agency shall give interested parties opportunity for—the submission and consideration of facts, arguments, *offers of settlement,* or proposals of adjustment when time, the nature of the proceeding, and the public interest permit.[6]

As time went on, regulatory agencies developed a multitude of traditional processes, including rulemakings, paper hearings, and trial-type hearings before ALJs, to address a conflict between a regulated entity and those impacted by a proposed or actual action by the regulated entity. However, an agency's final decision on the merits of the participants' arguments may not end the conflict. A party that disagrees with a federal agency decision may continue its case in one of the District Courts of the United States or one of the United States Courts of Appeals.

The traditional processes have several things in common. They take time and require extensive resources; additionally, someone other than the involved parties will make the decision and instruct the parties how to proceed. Each party puts on its best case during the process. Although there may be a "winner" and a "loser," often neither party is entirely satisfied with the outcome. The parties are then left to implement the decision, whether they agree with it or not. Perhaps because of this, parties' implementation of the outcome resulting from a traditional process may lead to monitoring and enforcement actions that can prolong resolution. And, although some of these decisions are necessary (e.g., to establish precedent), the burden on the administrative and court systems can be costly. The trickle-down effects are considerable, with "vital economic interests . . . and business expansion . . . severely handicapped, and reforms necessary for the protection of workers and consumers . . . long postponed."[7] In short, reliance on traditional processes alone may not always serve the regulatory community. One important contributor is that "administrative procedures, initially developed as a safeguard against the threat of regulatory abuse, have come to mimic the judicial process, with inadequate regard for the flexibility available under existing statutes."[8]

One thing is certain: regulatory disputes between regulated entities and those impacted by the actions and decisions of these entities persist. Underscoring these disputes is the reality that there are differences resulting from "incompatible interests, goals, principles or feelings."[9] Differences may emanate from varying amounts of information or understanding of a problem, from priorities that do not align, and/or from varied perspectives on time frame or resources, as well as inconsistent access to information about a problem.[10] Differences may also emanate from different interpretations of agency rules, precedent, and policy. In the regulatory arena, these differences manifest themselves in disputes ranging from how best to regulate an industry given market forces to case-specific disputes that affect only those impacted by the action or proposed action of a regulated entity. The dynamic is complicated and is magnified by interdependent relationships, such as those between businesses (e.g., utilities) and customers who have an ongoing relationship or partnership.

We typically respond to disputes based on three factors: Who is right? (rights) Who is more powerful? (power) Or what do we need? (interests)[11] The response is critical, because that often determines the mechanism that we choose to manage and/or resolve the dispute. Traditional processes to resolve regulatory disputes often hover in the realm of rights or power and center around litigation. Undeniably, litigation is necessary and desired in some situations, to establish precedent or to get a definitive ruling on issues that, if not addressed, will continue to challenge the parties. In cases that do not involve a precedential question or pose the need for finality on an issue, litigation may not be the appropriate mechanism for resolving a regulatory conflict and addressing what parties need. Enter ADR.

ADR Processes

ADR encompasses processes for settling disputes without using courts or an agency (as utilized in traditional processes). With the exception of arbitration, ADR processes are collaborative and consensus-building, and they allow parties, through dialogue, to understand each other's issues and what is important to the other parties, with the assistance of a neutral third party. ADR allows the parties to develop more creative and expanded solutions than a court or regulatory agency legally may be allowed to order. ADR processes are confidential; that is, what is said in the ADR discussions is not shared in another forum unless the parties agree to do so. Because of this, parties may share ideas in an ADR session that they wouldn't share in a traditional, nonconfidential process. Usually, ADR procedures are thought to be less costly and more expeditious than traditional processes. For example, in contrast with litigation, ADR procedures generally do not involve testimony and depositions. Because parties craft their own solutions to meet their concerns, they are more likely to successfully implement a mutually acceptable solution.

One distinction between the traditional and the alternative processes is the disputing parties' role in the resolution process. In traditional processes, a third party external to the dispute (viz., an arbitrator, judge, or agency) makes a decision about the outcome of the dispute. In contrast, with ADR, the parties to the dispute jointly decide how their dispute will be resolved. In other words, the parties in an ADR process are in control of the outcome. Although this can be challenging, time-consuming, and daunting, the parties (as experts in their dispute) are well positioned to play this role.

But what are the processes that parties can use to take a central role in resolving their dispute? Before exploring the processes encompassed in the ADR Processes table (Table 1), we must first look at negotiation. This is an unassisted process that

TABLE 1. ADR Processes

TYPE*	DESCRIPTION
Conciliation	Fosters a productive dialogue to resolve differences
Facilitation	Improves the flow of information in a meeting; helps a group reach a decision or specific outcome
Mediation	Helps parties negotiate to reach an acceptable resolution of the issues in a dispute
Early Neutral Evaluation	Offers a nonbinding evaluation of the strengths and weaknesses of each party's case
Minitrial	Offers high-level decision makers the opportunity to hear the other parties present the merits of their case
Med-Arb	Combines mediation and arbitration
Nonbinding Arbitration	Involves a third party or panel rendering a nonbinding decision
Arbitration	Involves a third party or panel rendering a decision that is binding

* Each type involves a neutral third party.

involves direct interaction between parties to resolve their issues. In *The Mind and Heart of the Negotiator,* Leigh Thompson defines *negotiation* as "a decision-making process by which two or more people agree how to allocate scarce resources. . . . The presence of two or more people implies that the decision-making process is inherently interdependent—that is, what one party does affects the other party."[12] The concept of interdependence is an important one. A precursor to negotiation is a recognition that engagement with another party (or other parties) is the first step toward achieving a goal. What that engagement looks like will determine what goal(s) are achieved.

Stephen Frenkel characterizes the purpose of negotiation as a necessary back and forth: "the entire purpose of a negotiation is to create and extract as much value as possible from the *combined* experience or resources of all players. . . . After all, if either party could go it alone, why would they be negotiating with each other in the first place?"[13] In a negotiation, disputing parties have control over the process they use to reach agreement and the outcome they ultimately achieve. It is the least costly resolution option because there is no third party involved. However, to be effective, negotiating parties must be equipped to identify and examine issues, explore ideas for resolution, navigate challenges, and reach agreement. Sometimes parties are successful in this regard. When they are not, a third party may be brought in to help parties make progress and negotiate more

BOX 1. CONCILIATION IN PRACTICE

Arizona Public Service and Navajo Tribal Utility Authority

In 1999, Arizona Public Service Company (APS) filed an unexecuted transmission service agreement, which required the Navajo Tribal Utility Authority (NTUA) to make improvements to transmission facilities located on Navajo tribal lands. The NTUA asserted that, although it had the obligation to maintain the lines, the improvements APS sought were unnecessary due to the small loads involved and the unique nature of service provided within NTUA's jurisdiction. The FERC ordered a hearing but held it in abeyance to allow for settlement negotiations.[1] A FERC Dispute Resolution Service (DRS)[2] representative met with the parties, and, as a result, the parties agreed to unassisted negotiations that, within sixty days, led to a settlement, which the Commission accepted.

All information is public in all the examples in this chapter. The authors of this book served as the third-party neutral in the examples in this chapter.

1. *Arizona Pub. Serv. Co.*, 88 FERC ¶ 61,183 at 61,595 (1999).
2. The FERC Dispute Service is an independent unit in FERC that provides alternative dispute resolution services to parties for FERC-related matters and is discussed in detail in a later chapter.

effectively. Involvement of a third party brings us to the processes in the ADR Processes table. Each is discussed below.

Conciliation

Conciliation fosters a positive dialogue between parties to restore damaged relationships or even meet for the first time. The neutral third party, or conciliator, will work individually and collectively with parties to encourage communication and spark productive dialogue. This is not as simple and straightforward as it sounds. Parties to a dispute often find it difficult to "hear" the other side or to understand the other side's perspective. The conciliator can help to bridge this gap.

Initially, the conciliator may act as a shuttle diplomat, exchanging messages and exploring perceptions and misperceptions among the parties. The conciliator may serve as a sounding board for strong emotions, giving the parties an opportunity to vent and sort through what they are feeling so that they will be able to engage productively. The goal of conciliation is to build trust between parties and enhance

BOX 2. FACILITATION IN PRACTICE

TEPPCO—Throughput of Propane in Kentucky

In December 2000, Kentucky Governor Paul Patton asked the FERC to explore the possibility of increasing the throughput of propane into Kentucky on the TEPPCO line because of a short supply during an extended cold period. In January 2001, the DRS facilitated a meeting with representatives of the Governor, TEPPCO, the Kentucky Propane Gas Association, the Kentucky Petroleum Marketers, and distributors. The purpose of the meeting was to discuss the current situation in Kentucky, how TEPPCO allocates capacity on its propane pipeline, and ways to get more propane into Kentucky. Because of the meeting, the participants obtained a fuller understanding of the limitations of service but found a way to ship more propane into the state. The participants also recognized that, for the long term, the group needed to work together to avoid similar situations in future cold years. As a result of the successful DRS facilitation, the Commission was able to respond quickly and effectively to the pressing need to get more propane to Kentucky. At the same time, using minimal resources and funds, the Commission avoided a formal inquiry, which would have involved many participants from different states, several filings and data inquiries, and countless meetings.

their commitment to work together. As with negotiation, in conciliation, the parties retain control of the substantive outcome of their dispute. And, although a third party is engaged to help them make progress, the parties largely retain control over the process to achieve their goals. This method is often used prior to or in tandem with facilitation or mediation (both described below).

Facilitation

Facilitation is a process involving the use of a third party neutral to improve the flow of information in a meeting and/or to help a group reach a decision or specific outcome regarding an issue. As with negotiation and conciliation, in facilitation the parties to the dispute retain control of the substantive outcome. The facilitator serves as the neutral process manager, providing structure and tools to ensure information exchange and meeting progress. Often facilitators will reach out to parties in advance of a meeting to understand perspectives and gather information about priority topics.

At the meeting, and any subsequent meetings, the facilitator generally ensures that the agenda for the meeting encompasses all priority topics and presents an overview of how the meeting will progress. Throughout this process, the facilitator actively listens, records perspectives and decisions, summarizes what has been done and what is outstanding, and solicits feedback from parties. The process is interactive and the parties are encouraged to speak out if they feel there are unaddressed issues or if the meeting structure is not effective. Following the meeting, the facilitator generally provides a meeting overview and reminds parties of action items and time frames.

Mediation

Mediation is a process involving a third party, the mediator, who helps parties negotiate an acceptable resolution of the issues in dispute. Mediators are neutral, with no power to make a decision or tell people what to do. Mediators do not advocate for either side; they advocate for a fair process. Mediators employ tools such as active listening to identify the issues and, more importantly, to explore with parties what they value (i.e., why they want what they say they want).

The directiveness a mediator employs depends on whether a mediator is facilitative or evaluative. A facilitative mediator focuses primarily on structuring a process through which parties can reach a mutually acceptable resolution. "The facilitative mediator does not make recommendations to the parties, give his or her advice or opinion as to the outcome of the case, or predict what a court would do in the case."[14] On the other hand, an evaluative mediator gets more involved in substance. "An evaluative mediator assists the parties in reaching resolution by pointing out the weaknesses of their cases and predicting what a judge or jury would likely do. An evaluative mediator might make recommendations to the parties as to the outcome of the issues."[15] A mediator could employ either approach at different times in the mediation depending on the situation. No matter where a mediator falls along the facilitative-evaluative scale, the goal of mediation is the same: to assist parties in structuring communication so they better understand the issues in dispute and the different perspectives on these issues.

Mediators meet with parties jointly and/or separately to understand how their goals relate to the other side's goals: Do they align? Are they different but not in conflict? Are they incompatible? Mediators work with parties to understand their priorities and to brainstorm separately and collectively about how to achieve

BOX 3. MEDIATION IN PRACTICE

Movement of Crude Petroleum When Its Quality Is at Issue

On March 31, 2004, Chevron Pipe Line Company (Chevron) filed a tariff covering the movement of crude petroleum into its Empire Terminal in Plaquemines Parish, Louisiana, to make explicit the requirement that crude petroleum transported on this line be sweet crude (i.e., crude petroleum with a sulfur content of less than or equal to 0.5 percent by weight). Chevron asserted that it maintained the common stream on its pipeline as a sweet stream, consistent with its tariffs. Chevron said that accepting sour crude into its facilities would change the facilities' character and cause financial detriment to it and to other customers shipping sweet crude on the same system.

Marathon Oil Company, Marathon Pipe Line, Devon Louisiana Corporation, and Spinnaker Exploration Company filed interventions and protests. Marathon Oil argued that Chevron's proposal would adversely affect delivery of Marathon Oil's production to downstream markets and was unjust, unreasonable, and discriminatory. Devon and Spinnaker noted that there was no previous restriction on the sulfur content and Chevron ignored reasonable alternatives to this restriction.

In its order on March 31, 2004, the FERC said it encouraged the production and marketing of new crude oil and that it could require a pipeline to provide transportation but would not require a pipeline to accept new volumes of crude oil that would change the historic operating conditions on the pipeline and cause financial detriment to other shippers. The Commission further observed that the financial impacts on shippers were unknown and that, if shippers of crude wished to transport their crude, they must pay for any additional facilities or other accommodations that may be necessary to accomplish this transportation without degrading the existing sweet common stream.[1] The Commission noted that the parties had been negotiating for over eighteen months without reaching an agreement and referred the case to FERC's DRS.

The DRS mediator worked with the parties, and within six months, by September 2004, the parties filed a settlement to resolve their issues. In October 2004, the Commission approved the settlement.[2]

1. *Chevron Pipe Line Company,* 106 FERC ¶ 61,338 (2004).
2. *Chevron Pipe Line Company,* 109 FERC ¶ 61,116 (2004).

the high-priority goals for both sides. Once parties have identified options for doing so, the parties (with the help of the mediator) evaluate their options and build a foundation for settlement. Mediators often engage in "reality testing" with parties—encouraging them to think about what the case will look like if it does not settle and, specifically, what they might expect if the case proceeds along a more traditional path. In mediation, as with conciliation and facilitation, the parties have a say in the process and they employ their expertise in the matter—and in what is important to them—to craft an outcome.

As we move down the list of processes in the table, the role of the neutral third party becomes more evaluative.

Early Neutral Evaluation

In early neutral evaluation (ENE), the early neutral evaluator is an impartial third party who offers a nonbinding evaluation for the parties on the strengths and weaknesses of their cases. The neutral evaluator is bound by confidentiality. ENE may be useful when parties are stuck on the value of their respective cases, the relevancy or meaning of pertinent technical information, or factual issues. The parties jointly select the early neutral evaluator and the approach the evaluator employs. The early neutral evaluator is an expert with relevant legal, substantive, and/or technical expertise or experience in the disputed areas.

The evaluator might meet separately with each party or jointly with all parties to answer questions. Then the evaluator provides, either separately or jointly, an objective opinion on the issues they were asked to address. The neutral evaluator can equip both sides with additional information to assess their potential liabilities moving forward.

Minitrial

A minitrial is a process where each party presents its position to a panel of decision makers. As with ENE, minitrials can be effective when parties are stuck on the value of their cases, relevancy or meaning of information, facts, or legal issues. The rationale behind a minitrial is that if the decision makers are directly informed of the merits of each party's case, they will be better prepared to successfully engage in settlement discussions. Though a minitrial can have different formats, it often includes decision makers and the neutral sitting on a panel and directly hearing

BOX 4. ENE IN PRACTICE

City and County of San Francisco v. Pacific Gas and Electric Company

On June 29, 2005, the City and County of San Francisco (the City) filed with FERC a complaint and motion for issuance of an order to show cause against Pacific Gas and Electric Company (PG&E). The City was disputing PG&E bills and charges and PG&E billing for services under the Interconnection Agreement (IA) between PG&E and the City. The City requested that FERC enjoin PG&E from invoking the arbitration provisions contained in the IA. PG&E challenged the City's billing issues and asserted that the IA required resolution through arbitration.

Prior to filing the complaint, the City discussed ADR options with the Director of FERC's DRS. In its answer to the City's complaint, PG&E agreed to meet with FERC's DRS and the City to discuss ADR, with the understanding that PG&E did not waive any rights under the IA.

On July 25, 2005, the City and PG&E met with the Director of FERC's DRS to discuss the available ADR options. These discussions led to an agreement to stay arbitration pending completion of (1) a DRS-sponsored ENE and (2) mediation with a private mediator. In September, the City and PG&E participated in an ENE with a high-level former FERC attorney serving as the early neutral evaluator. Following the ENE, the City and PG&E participated in a mediation with a retired San Francisco Superior Court judge serving as the mediator. On October 7, 2005, the City and PG&E agreed to a settlement, which FERC later approved.[1]

1. See *By Letter Order*, 115 FERC ¶61,106 (2006). See also, PG&E v. City of San Francisco, 120 FERC ¶ 61,182 (2007).

what each party thinks about the case. The presentations can take many forms, including legal arguments by counsel, witness testimony, and company officials' perspectives. The presentations encapsulate the critical elements of each party's position and provide pertinent information for the other side, which may impact their motivation and willingness to settle. The neutral may be a mediator, a former judge, or an individual versed in the relevant law or subject matter. The neutral explains the process and maintains order throughout the presentations. After the presentations, the parties decide if they want to negotiate on their own or request the neutral to play a role. The neutral could provide a nonbinding advisory ruling on

BOX 5. MINITRIAL IN PRACTICE

Trans Alaska Pipeline

In 1989, the owners[1] of the Trans Alaska Pipeline (TAPS)[2] filed with FERC to increase the rates it charged customers to transport oil through its facilities by approximately 120 million dollars to recover costs to repair corrosion on the pipeline. The State of Alaska (Alaska) and Petro Star Inc. challenged the lawfulness of the corrosion-related costs. Alaska asserted that the costs were due to defective design, construction, and maintenance of the pipeline. On December 29, 1989, FERC set the case for hearing before an ALJ.

At the first prehearing conference held on February 8, 1990, the assigned ALJ, Judge Lotis, suggested that the parties consider an ADR approach. He later issued a notice encouraging the parties to consider using an ADR process. He informed the parties that it was unlikely that a hearing could commence until sometime in 1992, given the need for extensive discovery and trial preparation. Judge Lotis noted that the parties litigated earlier for more than seven years (1977–1985) over the rates applying to the shipment of oil on TAPs. He observed:

> Apart from these direct settlement costs, it is reasonable to assume that the case must have exacted enormous indirect costs on all parties. Litigation can hardly be an economically productive activity. Productivity was presumably affected as the owners' management had to divert their attention from operations and projects to the oversight of ongoing litigation. Similarly, regulators concerned primarily with the formulation and implementation of state and national energy policy matters had to allocate considerable resources to a case-specific problem. On both sides, technical experts such as accountants, economists, engineers, and geologists had to be diverted from current assignments either to participate actively in the case or to supervise or coordinate the work of the outside consultants. Certainly, the litigation could not have had a positive effect on the trust and confidence essential for a mutually beneficial working relationship between Alaska and the TAPS owners.[3]

In his notice, Judge Lotis noted that at the prehearing conference, "the parties charted a course for this proceeding which, if left unaltered, would take them on a journey over familiar waters—déjà vu 1977–1985."[4] The parties subsequently entered into a minitrial agreement (ADR Agreement) that provided for a panel consisting of a neutral, who was a former judge on the US Ninth Circuit Court of Appeals, a delegate from FERC trial staff, and a representative from each party. The minitrial was to educate the parties' decision makers and the neutral as to the strength of each party's case. This arrangement was also deemed a settlement negotiation, and, thus, the participants were subject to strict confidentiality rules. The proposed ADR Agreement was certified to the Commission for approval. On November 28, 1990, FERC issued an order approving the ADR Agreement.[5]

The minitrial was a two-step process. Step 1 consisted of abbreviated presentations that were preceded by briefs (not to exceed twenty-five pages). The presentations could be made in any form and were not subject to rules of evidence except those pertaining to privileged communications and attorney work product. Any member of the minitrial panel could ask questions of counsel or other persons appearing on a party's behalf. Following the minitrial, the parties would attempt to negotiate an acceptable solution. If these unassisted negotiations failed, the neutral who sat on the panel was available to present his or her views regarding the strength and weaknesses of each party's case and the probable outcome should the matter be tried before FERC and the Alaska Public Utility Commission. Following receipt of the neutral's views, the neutral could move into step 2—mediation—if requested by the parties. The mediation sessions could be joint or separate. The minitrial lasted less than two days. The parties immediately engaged in unassisted negotiations that were successful. On February 19, 1992, the Commission approved the settlement, finding that it constituted a fair and reasonable resolution of the issues raised. The Commission further stated that the settlement represented an enormous achievement on the part of Judge Lotis and the parties.[6]

1. Amerada Hess Pipeline Corporation, ARCO Pipeline Company, Exxon Pipeline Company, Mobil Alaska Pipeline Company, Phillips Alaska Pipeline Company, and Unocal Pipeline Company.

2. TAPS, an eight-hundred-mile oil pipeline, was constructed from the Prudhoe Bay Oil Field on the North Slope of Alaska to the Port of Valdez on Alaska's southern coast.

3. Notice Concerning the Use of Alternative Dispute Resolution Techniques, Amerada Hess Pipeline Co, Docket Nos. IS-11-000, et al., issued February 21, 1990, p. 2. The proposed ADR Agreement was certified to the Commission for approval on October 16, 1990. 53 FERC ¶ 63,004 (1990).

4. See Notice at page 3.

5. *Amerada Hess Pipeline Co, et al.*, 53 FERC ¶ 61,266 (1990). This marked the first time that parties in a FERC proceeding developed a formal ADR mechanism for resolving their differences.

6. *Amerada Hess Pipeline Co, et al.*, 58 FERC ¶ 61,173 at 61,521 (1992).

the merits or settlement options, or the neutral could transition to a mediator role. As mentioned above, although there is no set model for a minitrial, two elements are essential to the success of the process: (1) limitations on the time and scope and (2) participation of high-level corporate officials who have the authority to enter into a settlement. Both of these elements were present in the minitrial example in this chapter.

Arbitration

Lastly, there is arbitration, where a third party or panel renders a decision that can be binding on the parties. This is the process that is most like litigation. In arbitration, the parties relinquish control of the process and outcome that they wielded in negotiation and the other ADR processes. With that said, there have been permutations to the arbitration process over the years. First, there is the mediation–arbitration amalgam, or *med-arb*. With med-arb, the parties first use mediation to settle their dispute. If they are not successful or if outstanding issues remain, the case proceeds to arbitration, where the arbitrator renders a binding decision on the entire dispute or the remaining issues. Approaches to med-arb differ, but typically parties opt to select a separate mediator and arbitrator rather than use the same person as the neutral in the mediation and in the arbitration. This approach preserves the distinction between the two roles and gives the parties the opportunity to freely explore the potential for a mediated settlement without fearing that what they say may impact an arbitrated award.

Second, there is nonbinding arbitration, in which an arbitrator or arbitration panel renders a nonbinding decision about the issues in dispute. The parties usually agree on the arbitrator selection process, whether they are selecting a single arbitrator or a panel of arbitrators. Nonbinding arbitration may be inviting for parties who are interested in a definitive determination of their dispute but do not necessarily want to be bound by it. With that said, the nonbinding determination may have considerable impact.

Finally, there is binding arbitration, which is most like litigation because the arbitrator or panel of arbitrators renders a binding decision. As in nonbinding arbitration, the parties usually agree on the arbitrator selection process, whether they are selecting a single arbitrator or a panel of arbitrators. Typically, the parties present their cases and the arbitrator considers that information along with written

BOX 6. MED-ARB IN PRACTICE

Lavand & Lodge and New England Independent System Operator

Lavand & Lodge filed a complaint against the New England Independent System Operator (NEISO). In its complaint, Lavand & Lodge asked the FERC to order NEISO to refund the payment it made under NEISO's implementation of a settlement agreement in another docket. The settlement agreement, which involved many parties, required some parties to make payments and others to receive a share of those payments. Lavand & Lodge was one of the parties who paid but believed it paid in error. The Commission's DRS tried mediation, and, when the parties could not reach agreement, the DRS representative suggested that the parties go to binding arbitration, with a Commission ALJ serving as the arbitrator. The parties, wanting a quick resolution, agreed to this arrangement and agreed to abide by the ALJ/arbitrator's decision. The ALJ/arbitrator issued a final, binding decision less than two months after the FERC Chief Judge appointed the ALJ/arbitrator.[1]

1. See *Lavand & Lodge, LLC v. ISO New England Inc.*,126 FERC ¶ 63,005 (2009).

information before rendering an arbitration award. The award is binding on the parties.

Throughout this chapter, we have addressed the various processes that federal and state regulatory agencies employ. Understanding the range of processes to resolve disputes, from negotiation to mediation to litigation, is critical because it helps to inform decisions about which process is appropriate for the dispute at hand. There is no one process that is applicable every time; the key is fitting the process to the problem.[16] In the next chapter, we will explore ways to design a dispute resolution system that incorporates a range of ADR processes that do just that.

CHAPTER 2

Designing a Sustainable Dispute Resolution System

In chapter 1, we looked at the nature of conflict, recognizing that conflict, if managed effectively, can be an opportunity to maximize learning and promote positive change. In the complex state and federal regulatory realms, maximizing the opportunity of conflict necessitates a comprehensive understanding of the dispute dynamic of an organization, particularly those organizations that were created by law and have their own rules, regulations, and policies. Who are the stakeholders? What are the concerns? What are the challenges? What are the resolution practices to date? What works well? What could be improved? Understanding the dispute dynamic equips designers with the information to identify the problems and to craft or tweak an accessible and responsive dispute resolution program to address those problems. The end product is a system that equips all stakeholders with the information, skills, and options they need to manage their disputes.

Employing a comprehensive and systematic approach to dispute resolution requires a proactive orientation to conflict, rather than reactive responses. In the regulatory realm, with competing demands for time and money, devoting attention to present and future conflict may not feel like a priority. As Cathy Constantino and Christina Sickles Merchant point out in their seminal work, *Designing Conflict Management Systems,* "conflict . . . is viewed and managed in a piecemeal, ad hoc fashion, as isolated events."[1] In contrast, investment in a proactive approach enables regulatory entities to learn from past conflicts and manage and anticipate present and future conflicts. With a proactive approach, some conflicts may be avoided altogether.

The newly developed Voices of Value Model provides a roadmap for designing a dispute resolution system and prioritizing the voices of those impacted by regulatory disputes. It defines what they value and hope to achieve and informs the path to get there for present and future disputes. Including the voices of affected parties in designing a system heightens the possibility that it will be responsive, relevant, and useful for those it is designed to serve. It may also foster a commitment to the success and sustainability of the system: "If *you* build it, they may or may not use it. On the other hand, if *they* build it, they will use it."[2]

The key at the outset in designing or tweaking a system is to think about the stakeholder universe in the regulatory arena. This may include the regulators, the regulated and their customers, landowners, distributors, transmission providers, suppliers, and private and public interest groups. The next step is to involve representatives of potential constituencies in the design process. Anticipating potential obstacles to engaging constituencies and ways to overcome these obstacles are essential. An important question to ask throughout the systems design effort is whether there are parties not involved who may have the power to thwart or impact the process moving forward. If so, then those parties should be contacted, invited to participate, and encouraged to do so. Though this may seem laborious, the investment of time up front will reap dividends when a system is implemented that meets the needs of all potentially impacted constituencies.

A second step in building a system is conducting an analysis to understand the dispute landscape. What are the current disputes in the state and federal regulatory arenas? Which are most challenging and resource intensive? What are the categories of disputes and who is typically involved? How often do disputes emerge and what seems to be the cause? What are the costs of these disputes in management, staff, and legal time? Once the "state of conflict" is understood, the following questions may be explored: How are disputes handled now? What are the process options? Why are these the process options? Are there regulations or laws that dictate what the process options will be? What works well? What does not work well? What could be tweaked? What is the feedback to date?[3]

Once these preliminary questions are addressed, the stage is set to employ the Voices of Value roadmap to craft or tweak a dispute resolution system for the state and federal regulatory realms. The model is depicted in figure 1. As evidenced by the infographic, there are three phases in the Voices of Value Model: information, visioning, and implementation.

FIGURE 1. Voices of Value Model.

Our Process

INFORMATION

Values encompass:
- What is valued by the parties—in this process and in general?

Outcomes & Opportunities encompass:
- What is the outcome that parties want to achieve and how do we make the most of this opportunity to get there?

VISIONING

Ideas encompass:
- What are thoughts on how to move forward?

Collaboration encompasses:
- How do we work together to translate my ideas and your ideas into responsive and jointly agreeable solutions?

IMPLEMENTATION

Empowerment encompasses:
- What needs to happen and who needs to be empowered—with skills, with resources—to translate ideas and solutions into action?

Sustainability encompasses:
- How do we ensure responsibility and accountability so that solutions and changes sustain over time?

Information

The first phase, building on the information gathered in the preliminary analysis to map stakeholders and analyze disputes, consists of two components: (*1*) *values and* (*2*) *outcome and opportunities.* The first encompasses working with the identified stakeholders to understand what they value and need in a dispute resolution system. What are their goals? What are their concerns? Is the sole goal to achieve resolution or are there ancillary goals, such as equipping impacted entities with the skills and tools not only to manage disputes but also to prevent disputes? What is important to the varied stakeholders?

The second component, *outcome and opportunity,* starts with learning more about the outcome stakeholders hope to achieve. This requires a future-focused approach. Looking ahead, what does success look like? Does success translate into fewer disputes? Time and cost savings? Improved relationships? How will success be measured? How will information about operations and cost savings be collected and disseminated? Leaders in dispute systems design suggest the evaluation process be developed at the outset rather than at the end of the design effort: this "ensures that the evaluation is measuring progress continuously in accordance with the system's defined goals and objectives."[4] Thinking intentionally about and incorporating evaluation measures into the design process enhance the possibility that the program design will reflect and realize the desired outcome.

Stakeholders to a dispute systems design process have a unique opportunity to craft the process they will use to manage and resolve their disputes. But how can an agency or organization make the most of this opportunity? Is there momentum now to make changes? If not, what information is needed to generate it? If so, how can that momentum be directed to crafting a system that will sustain itself?

Visioning

The second phase, visioning, is informed by the data gathered about values and about outcome and opportunity. It has two components: *ideas and collaboration.* The first component, *ideas,* encompasses stakeholders' views on how to move forward and achieve the outcome they envisage. This process involves brainstorming. Through brainstorming, stakeholders reflect on the current system and strategize about changes. How might the current resolution options be tweaked or enhanced to meet the needs of the stakeholders and achieve the goals of the system? Given the nature of disputes in the regulatory realm, for example, do parties want more opportunity for feedback on their litigation exposure prior to or during settlement discussions? If so, then having the option of a common "evaluator" to give each party "independently a frank assessment of the issues" may be helpful in informing how parties evaluate a case and craft a settlement offer.[5] Or perhaps the different perspectives could be "submitted to an agreed 'expert' with minimal documentation and an agreement to abide by the expert's choice between the alternatives."[6] The purpose of this component is to be thorough and creative. The discussion is structured through the lens of the possible: in an ideal world, what would the optimal dispute resolution system look like?

The second component is *collaboration* among stakeholders. Collaboration encompasses working together to consider all ideas and to assess what is important and feasible. Applying criteria can be helpful. Criteria define the general characteristics that a system should have without prescribing a specific model. Stakeholders can be encouraged to think about the different visions of an optimal dispute resolution system that have been expressed through this process—and how those might piggyback or align. The outcome of collaboration is to identify the building blocks of a responsive and sustainable system.

Implementation

The third phase, implementation, is probably the most important phase, comprising two components: *empowerment and sustainability.* The effort to get to this phase is considerable, and the work done here will ensure the stakeholders and other interested parties achieve what they articulated and imagined in the information and visioning phases. *Empowerment* encompasses examining the solutions and determining what is needed to translate these solutions into action. Are there financial considerations? Are there bureaucratic hurdles to be overcome? Is training necessary for those personnel who will implement the system? Is outreach necessary to alert stakeholders about the components of the system and the best ways to access those components? Ensuring that these questions are answered and addressed will equip those spearheading the effort with the necessary tools to build a successful system.

The final component in this phase (and in the model) is *sustainability.*

Sustainability encompasses incorporating mechanisms to ensure responsibility and accountability so that the dispute resolution system sustains itself over time. Key elements are feedback and evaluation, which require the parties to reflect on the process goals and to interact with those who will utilize the system. Are parties satisfied after participating in an alternative process? Are they inclined to participate again? Are there things about the system that worked particularly well? Are there resources that would have enabled them to take better advantage of the system? Are there things about the system that did not work well and might deter them from utilizing an alternative process in the future? Learning about what is working and not working will inform investments in the system that will, hopefully, position it to continue. Also integral to sustainability are accountability and responsibility. Who is the point person or point office for overseeing the system and implementing changes necessary to keep it responsive and relevant?

At the end of the day, the true test is whether the process satisfies the needs of those it is designed to serve. Jonathan Raab noted in his book, *Using Consensus Building to Improve Utility Regulation,* that we need to look at participants when determining the success of an alternative process, because "ultimately, the success of a consensus-based process must be tied to how well the substantive outcome satisfied the various interests in society."[7]

The key with this model is to customize a system that reflects and responds to the problems, challenges, and opportunities of a particular state or federal regulatory entity. Customization is important because each case, issue, and sphere is different and there is no one answer or avenue for addressing the range of complex challenges. Rather, a menu of options is needed to respond to the needs of the parties. Nevertheless, experience has demonstrated a handful of components to be integral to the sustainability and success of any system: leadership, funding and resources, flexibility, training and outreach, and tracking and evaluation. Each is discussed in the following sections.

Leadership

Since support must come from the top, having leadership commitment to alternative dispute resolution approaches is one of the most important ingredients of a successful ADR Program. Leaders play multiple roles. First, they are champions of ADR process options, extolling the benefits of, and perhaps even incentivizing, ADR use.[8] Leaders are knowledgeable, are well versed in ADR process options, and are

BOX 7. CONSENSUS-BASED APPROACH IN PRACTICE

Natural Gas Pipeline Route and a Concerned Community

A prime example of the link between a consensus-based process and societal interests can be found in a well-publicized 2002 natural gas pipeline certificate proceeding in New York for the Millennium pipeline. FERC issued an interim order to construct and operate a 424-mile pipeline, starting at Lake Erie, connecting to Consolidated Edison's high-pressure line in Mount Vernon, New York. The order, however, did not certify a specific pipeline route through Mount Vernon because citizens opposed the construction of the pipeline through their community. The citizens claimed that the pipeline was too dangerous for a densely-populated city and was far too close to an elementary school, a community center, residential housing, and a hospital. Opponents of the line also asserted that the route through Mount Vernon was targeted because it was a community with a high percentage of minority residents. They expressed concerns about the environmental and economic impact, safety, and environmental justice. FERC requested that Millennium, elected officials, and interested parties and citizens in Mount Vernon negotiate an alternative route; FERC Dispute Resolution Service (DRS)[1] neutrals were brought in to mediate this negotiation. Over the next three months, mediators from DRS worked regularly with the parties, resulting in an agreement between Millennium and the Mount Vernon mayor and city council. The agreement was lauded by the community, the Millennium Pipeline Company, Mount Vernon elected officials, and both US senators from New York. The agreement positioned the company and the community to continue to work closely together as the pipeline work progressed.

1. The FERC Dispute Service is an independent unit in FERC that provides alternative dispute resolution services to parties for FERC-related matters and is discussed in detail in a later chapter.

attuned to plucking cases that are appropriate for ADR. Leaders secure funding and oversee the screening of cases. Leaders are shepherds, fostering the responsiveness and use of process options for a successful program, collecting valuable feedback, and tweaking the program as necessary. Finally, leaders—from agency heads, to individuals selected to spearhead the ADR Program, to office directors—must maintain high enthusiasm and support for the ADR Program, sharing successes and lessons learned.

Funding and Resources

Dedicated funding and resources to develop and operate ADR Programs are also critical ingredients in a sustainable and successful ADR Program. Funding and resources serve two purposes. First, an ADR budget and ADR staff enable those spearheading the program to fund and support the training, outreach, and development that ensure there are boots on the ground to manage requests and resolution processes. However, it is of equal importance that dedicated funding and staff provide legitimacy to an ADR Program. When leadership dedicates funding and staff, it shows commitment to integrating ADR process options into business operations. At the same time, dedicated funding and staff enable an ADR office to operate independently of other entities within the agency or organization. This sends a message to potential users that the processes are truly separate and independent from agency decision makers or organization operations. Perceptions matter, and the perception of separation and independence can set a tone at the outset of an ADR process that will carry through to a successful conclusion. Also, dedicated funding gives agency ADR specialists the ability to conduct ADR at the site of the dispute, which will provide greater incentive for decision makers from the parties to participate in the process.

Flexibility

Flexibility is another key ingredient of a successful and sustainable ADR Program. It manifests in various ways. First, the process itself must be flexible. From unassisted negotiation to arbitration with a combination of processes in between, options must be provided to reflect and address the disputes and needs of the parties.

Second, the entry point for dispute resolution must be flexible. The goal is to commence a process early, which some view as the best time for parties to collect facts, consider exposure, and think about strategy.[9] Moreover, commencing a process early may be advantageous because parties have not had as much opportunity to dig into their positions and take ownership of their "must haves." Thus, they may be more amenable to settlement. With that said, parties should also be enabled and encouraged to initiate an ADR process at any point leading up to litigation and even after litigation has started. They may need time up front to understand the dynamics of the case and the litigation risks before they consider settlement. They should not be precluded from engaging in ADR but rather encouraged to participate no matter where they are in another process. Participants must also be informed that engaging in ADR does not mean they forego their procedural rights if ADR negotiations fail.

Third, there must be flexibility in the structure and operation of the ADR process, from the selection of the neutral to additional resources that should be incorporated into a process. Energy regulatory cases are a breed unto themselves, often with multiple parties and highly complex issues, which can complicate negotiations and make settlements costlier. When bringing in a neutral, whether a facilitator, mediator, or settlement judge, parties will need to consider whether they want someone with a firm grasp of the critical technical issues to play that role.[10] Parties will also need to consider the related issue of the use of scientific and technical experts as part of the neutral team. This is important because facilitating collaboration to gather relevant data and foster a common understanding of the facts can lay the groundwork for agreement. Where there is an actual or perceived imbalance of power, subject-matter and technical experts can also help to level the playing field, particularly when one of the parties may be weaker than the other and could be disadvantaged throughout the dispute resolution process, heightening the risk of a potentially unfair agreement. For example, in a highly technical energy dispute between a landowner and a company, the company may have greater access to information, resources, and representation. An expert can share information and answer questions from both sides to balance this situation.

Training and Outreach

Training and outreach are also essential ingredients in a successful and sustainable ADR Program. Different training programs could be geared toward different audiences. The first training program might be geared toward potential users from the regulatory community, ranging from parties to company representatives to attorneys. This training program could focus on program mechanics, providing information on what to expect in an ADR process, from initiating ADR, to selecting a neutral, to navigating the process.[11] For stakeholders who are not familiar with ADR, this can be especially useful. Some designers suggest including a demonstration or videotape showing an actual ADR proceeding so users will have a reference point for what to expect.[12]

Another training program might be geared toward the staff who will coordinate the ADR Program and processes. This training program could encompass the ADR

Program overview, procedures, and guidelines governing ADR work; basic skills development critical for those on the ADR front lines, including communication skills and dispute resolution theory;[13] and essential elements of the program, such as confidentiality.

Another training program might be geared toward ADR professionals who will serve as neutrals, including potential facilitators, mediators, fact finders, and arbitrators.[14] This training program could encompass dispute resolution theory and practice with extensive opportunities to role-play the skills required to serve as a neutral. Though nothing substitutes for gaining the hands-on experience in a case, role-playing provides neutrals with some risk-free practice opportunities and a frame of reference for what it feels like in this role.

Outreach will be an ongoing process. The key will be to keep potential users, leaders, and champions informed and aware of the availability, relevancy, and results of the program. Initially, the goal of outreach is to introduce stakeholders to new (and improved) ADR process options. If the development and/or improvement of the dispute resolution program was accomplished through an inclusive and participatory design process, then the outreach must incorporate reference to what was heard and the ways that input is reflected in the program that has been developed. These outreach efforts may also address both what ADR is and what it is not.[15]

Some stakeholders resist mediation (or other ADR processes) because they believe someone will tell them what to do. These stakeholders need to be educated about the process and the neutral, impartial, non-decisional role of the mediator. The preliminary outreach effort also should encompass an overview of the ADR process options, the criteria used when evaluating whether a case is appropriate for ADR, instances where ADR is not appropriate, how to learn more about ADR, and how to initiate it in an organization or agency.[16] Later outreach efforts may incorporate lessons learned, success stories, a skills overview, and an opportunity for ADR coordinators to field questions about the program.

Tracking and Evaluation

Tracking and evaluation are also critical ingredients in a successful and sustainable ADR Program. A rigorous evaluation of an ADR Program, first and foremost, captures whether the program meets the needs of those it is designed to serve. One way to do this is to continually gather feedback on the process options and outcomes.

This provides critical information to program administrators regarding what is working well and what needs to be tweaked, informing them about immediate changes to enhance the experience of future users.

ADR Program evaluation also attempts to capture quantitative data, particularly regarding the time and money saved by participating in a dispute resolution process. However, this is not a straightforward calculation. The analysis "must extend beyond the . . . immediate proceeding [and] incorporate: savings associated with any reduced subsequent litigation, including appeals to the courts, as well as any savings associated with implementation of the settlement."[17] This may be difficult to capture, but looking at the ripple effect of successful dispute resolution processes can be informative and powerful. Having crafted a resolution to their dispute, parties to an ADR process are more likely to embrace implementation and may be more inclined to use collaborative processes to resolve future conflicts.

Though more difficult, it is also worthwhile to attempt to capture qualitative data through ADR Program evaluations. Questions related to qualitative matters get to the less tangible, but perhaps more powerful, benefits of alternative processes, including the following: Were the final remedies, plans, and policies easier to implement because the parties used a consensus-building process? Did the decisions achieved through ADR represent a substantive improvement over decisions that may have been achieved through a traditional process? The qualitative evaluation is informative because it helps to capture the benefits of those processes that achieve settlement and those that do not. Consensus processes cannot be judged by settlement alone—because the process to move toward consensus, even if unsuccessful, may be beneficial for several reasons.[18] Parties are educated about their own case, gaining a more realistic understanding of their prospects, and about what is important to the other parties. Even if resolution is not reached, parties may agree to resolve or drop certain issues before moving forward in a traditional process. The parties may also establish a more constructive and communicative rapport, which will help them navigate the case and help them with their interactions in the future (if they have an ongoing relationship).[19]

Pilot Program

Experience has also demonstrated that, even with a system that integrates the key components of leadership, funding and resources, flexibility, training and outreach, and tracking and evaluation, finding the right combination of options to include on a dispute resolution menu is daunting. One approach, to minimize the enormity of the task, is to start with a pilot program.[20]

The pilot program serves several purposes. It can minimize concerns about bringing change to a system that, though not perfect, may be familiar and acceptable to those who use it. The commitment to the pilot program can be for a defined time period, with a defined budget, thus providing an opportunity to commit to the program without an overwhelming initial investment of time or resources. A pilot program gives the dispute system designers, champions, and stakeholders a chance to try something new "with relatively low cost and low risk."[21] Perhaps more importantly, the pilot program also gives the designers, champions, and stakeholders a built-in reflection period—when the pilot ends, they have important feedback on where the system works well and where it can be enhanced to meet the needs of those it is designed to serve.

Summary

The end product of a dispute systems design effort is a system to manage and resolve disputes in a manner that is responsive to stakeholder needs in the regulatory conflict arena. Through the dispute systems design process, stakeholders may look at disputes and resolution mechanisms differently, may talk through differences in a constructive and creative way, and may be ready to recognize and seize those opportunities to jointly and proactively address their differences and resolve their conflicts. Though the goal is for disputants to use the well-designed system, it is hoped that the systems design process itself may equip stakeholders with the skills and tools to address their concerns early on and prevent conflict.

CHAPTER 3

Ensuring Dispute Resolution System Integrity

In chapter 2, we discussed the process of designing, implementing, and sustaining a successful ADR system. Equally important to success is incorporating ethical standards and safeguards that ensure the integrity of the dispute resolution system for those who operate within it.

Ethical Standards and Safeguards: Regulatory Agency

Ethical standards and institutional safeguards are intertwined, acting in tandem to instill confidence in the dispute resolution program, processes, and neutrals. Ethical standards apply to the regulatory agency's dispute resolution system, when it is developed and when it is implemented, and to the neutrals involved in the processes.

When developing a dispute resolution program for its constituency, regulators are responsible for creating a program that conforms with the agency's mission and follows the agency's statutory authority. The form of the dispute resolution program will vary depending on the mission and statutory authority of the regulating authority. For example, the mission of the Michigan Public Service Commission (MPSC) is to protect the public by ensuring safe, reliable, and accessible energy and telecommunications services at reasonable rates for Michigan's residents.[1] To assist consumers in resolving issues with their utility provider, the MPSC developed and implemented a comprehensive consumer dispute resolution program, with customer assistance at its core.[2] This program is discussed in chapter 8.

In addition, the regulator may encourage the development of dispute resolution programs for entities it regulates. For example, FERC encouraged FERC-regulated transmission entities to include internal dispute resolution provisions in their transmission tariffs. Responding to this encouragement, the Midwest Independent System Operator (MISO) Transmission Tariff and the MISO Business Practices Manual provide for a three-stage dispute resolution process encompassing informal discussion, mediation, and arbitration, if requested.[3] If informal discussion is unsuccessful, the parties move to mediation and, if mediation is not successful, to arbitration.

Lastly, the regulator may play a role in reviewing agreements. When negotiations result in a settlement, parties often have to file their settlement agreements with the regulatory authority if it alters a filed tariff, rate, terms and conditions of service, license condition, or any other requirement imposed on the regulated entity. The regulatory authority is responsible for reviewing settlement agreements using a standard the agency sets, such as being fair, reasonable, and in the public interest.

Ethical Standards and Safeguards: A Neutral's Responsibilities

Neutrals in dispute resolution proceedings must adhere to professional and statutory ethical standards. We view these standards through the lens of mediation.

Ethical guidelines for mediators derive from several sources. A few states, like Virginia, have a formal process for certifying mediators to practice in Virginia courts. The Supreme Court of Virginia manages the certification program and prescribes strict ethical requirements, which the Virginia-certified mediators must follow when mediating court-referred cases.

The federal government does not certify or license mediators. However, there are other sources of ethical guidance for mediators, particularly in regard to confidentiality, which is a foundational component of a dispute resolution process such as mediation. The Model Standards of Conduct for Mediators (Standards), promulgated in 1994 and revised in 2005 through a joint effort of the American Bar Association Section of Dispute Resolution, American Arbitration Association, and Association for Conflict Resolution, provide that the mediator shall maintain the confidentiality of all information obtained in mediation, unless otherwise agreed to by the parties or required by applicable law.[4] Confidentiality assures parties that what they say in the mediation will not be used in another forum, such as litigation or an administrative process, by either the mediator or the other parties.

In the federal realm, the 1990 ADR Act[5] established requirements regarding confidentiality of communications during ADR processes involving federal agencies, with the goal of balancing open government goals with the need for confidentiality in the ADR settlement process.[6] Some agencies have incorporated other safeguards to fortify this protection. For example, FERC went beyond the 1990 ADR Act and implemented additional confidentiality provisions, stating, "participants should feel free to be forthcoming and frank without fear that their statements may later be used against them . . . a neutral should be protected from being required to divulge such information."[7] Through Commission Rule 606,[8] FERC's confidentiality provisions apply to ADR proceedings established under Commission Rules 604 and 605.[9] Under Rule 606(a), a neutral in a dispute resolution proceeding cannot voluntarily disclose and cannot be required to disclose through discovery or compulsory process information concerning any dispute resolution communication or any communication provided in confidence to the neutral, unless one or more of the following conditions are met: all participants and the neutral consent in writing; the dispute resolution communication has already been made public; the communication is required by statute to be made public; and/or a court determines that the testimony or disclosure is necessary to achieve one of the following: preventing a manifest injustice, establishing a violation of law, and/or preventing harm to the public health or public safety of sufficient magnitude as to outweigh the integrity of dispute resolution proceedings in general by reducing the participants' confidence that their communications will remain confidential in future cases.[10]

Prohibitions against disclosure are closely related to confidentiality, and they fortify the confidential nature of the dispute resolution proceeding. For example, under FERC Rule 606(b), a participant cannot disclose information concerning any dispute resolution communication unless one of the four conditions in Rule 606(a) apply or the communication is relevant to determining the existence or meaning or the enforcement of an agreement or an award resulting from the proceeding. Under Rule 606(c),[11] any dispute resolution communication that is disclosed in violation of Rule 606(a) and (b) is not admissible in any proceeding.[12]

Also related to the institutional safeguard of confidentiality are provisions for parties to modify the standard related to confidential requests for disclosure. For example, under FERC Rule 606(d)(1),[13] participants to a dispute resolution proceeding may agree to alternative confidential procedures for disclosures by a neutral. The participants must inform the neutral of changes to the standard confidentiality rules before the dispute resolution proceeding begins. The modified confidentiality rules may not further restrict the confidential procedures otherwise

BOX 8. IMPROPER DISCLOSURE

Niagara Mohawk and Fourth Branch

In *Fourth Branch Assocs. (Mechanicville) v. Niagara Mohawk Power Corp.*,[1] Niagara Mohawk sent a letter to the New York State Historic Preservation Office (SHPO) with a copy to FERC. Niagara Mohawk attached documents to the letter that were produced in an unsuccessful mediation and were marked "confidential" and "privileged." Fourth Branch contended that, by sending the documents to the SHPO, Niagara Mohawk violated the Commission's Rules of Practice and Procedure barring the disclosure of such documents. Fourth Branch asked the Commission to strike the letter and attached documents from the Commission's record and to impose "appropriate sanctions" on Niagara Mohawk. In its response, Niagara Mohawk stated that it was entitled to do so in order to defend against Fourth Branch's use of confidential mediation documents to enlist the aid of the SHPO in Fourth Branch's dispute with Niagara Mohawk. The Commission struck from the record Niagara's documents, noting that the documents added nothing to the resolution of the basic issues posed in this case. The Commission did not impose sanctions.

All information in this example is public.

1. 89 FERC ¶ 61,194.

provided under Rule 606. Under FERC Rule 606(e),[14] if a participant receives a demand for disclosure of a dispute resolution communication, by way of discovery request or other legal process, the participant must make reasonable efforts to notify the neutral and other participants of the demand. If a participant is notified by another participant of a request for disclosure, that participant must object to the neutral disclosing the information within fifteen calendar days or else he or she waives any objection to the disclosure.

In addition to confidentiality, other ethical provisions articulated in the Standards guide mediator conduct, inform parties about what to expect from mediation, and promote public confidence in mediation as a process to resolve disputes. The most relevant provisions are self-determination, impartiality, conflict of interest, competence, and quality of process.

At its core, self-determination means that mediation should be a party-driven process. The mediator will serve as the process guide, but the parties are instrumental to the process and, more importantly, responsible for the outcome. With this in mind, the mediator should ensure that parties have the information they need up front to understand the process and voluntarily agree to engage in the process. Throughout the mediation, the mediator should check in with parties to make sure they are satisfied with the progress of the mediation. The most critical component of self-determination is that the solution be party-driven. The mediator will facilitate discussion, brainstorming, and option generation and evaluation between the parties; however, the parties—not the mediator—are the ultimate decision makers for their dispute. Mediation is a process that belongs to the parties and the solution is one that is developed by the parties who are, after all, the experts on the issues. Along the lines of self-determination, parties may agree to more-or-less stringent confidentiality terms for the mediation process and/or the settlement. For example, in a high-profile case, parties may agree to jointly draft a press release to issue after they reach agreement.

Impartiality is also important. The mediator shall conduct a mediation in an impartial manner, free from favoritism, bias, and prejudice. The mediator avoids conduct that gives the appearance of partiality. For example, the mediator shall ensure that each party is provided an adequate opportunity to participate in the process.

Conflict of interest is also important. A mediator cannot have a conflict of interest, or even the appearance of a conflict of interest, during or after a mediation. To avoid a conflict of interest, a mediator should ask questions to check for potential conflicts of interest, disclose potential conflicts, and withdraw from the mediation if a conflict of interest exists or develops that compromises his or her impartiality. For example, if a mediator owns stock in a company participating in the mediation, the mediator should disclose this to the parties before the process begins. If the parties perceive or the mediator feels that this connection will compromise neutrality, then the mediator must withdraw.

Mediators should have the training and skills to ensure that they are competent to serve as mediators and to meet the reasonable expectations of the parties. The mediator should candidly inform the parties of the mediator's background and experience and step away from the process if the parties question the mediator's competence.

A mediator shall conduct a mediation in a manner that ensures quality of process, focusing on timeliness, safety, participation, and procedural fairness. Mediators shall be clear about the process and their own role in the process. Mediators who are also attorneys should be clear about their role and should avoid giving legal advice. If the parties request that the mediator provide an evaluation of the case or of each party's case, then the mediator must ensure that parties are clear about the shift in roles from serving as a process guide to serving as an evaluator. The mediator should ensure that the parties have sufficient information to make an informed decision. Accordingly, the mediator should make the parties aware that they may consult other objective/impartial professionals to assist them in gathering and processing information.

Other Considerations

In addition to ethical considerations and safeguards, some agencies may institute further safeguards to buttress the integrity of the dispute resolution system. At FERC, one such institutional safeguard is separation of functions. In 1984, former acting FERC General Counsel Stephen R. Melton described the separation of functions rule in "Separation of Functions at the FERC: Does the Reorganization of the Office of General Counsel Mean What It Says?":

> Separation of functions is an administrative law doctrine that has as its purpose the protection of the independence and objectivity of the administrative-adjudicative function by restricting agency personnel with inconsistent functions, such as prosecution, investigation, or advocacy, from advising decision makers.[15]

For FERC personnel involved in a hearing as an ALJ, advocate, or witness, the separation of functions rule applies, pursuant to FERC Rule 2202, which provides:

> In any proceeding in which a Commission adjudication is made after hearing . . . no officer, employee, or agent assigned to work upon the proceeding or to assist in the trial thereof, in that or any factually related proceeding, shall participate or advise as to the findings, conclusion or decision, except as a witness or counsel in public proceedings.[16]

Rule 2202 applies to FERC's Dispute Resolution Service (DRS) specialists, because a settlement mediated by a DRS representative has the potential for Commission review. The DRS representative is prohibited from disclosing information from the mediation to non-parties and Commission employees. (DRS is an independent unit in FERC that provides alternative dispute resolution services to parties for FERC-related matters and is discussed in chapter 5.)

In its 2002 policy statement, the Commission elaborated on the relationship between dispute resolvers at the Commission and other staff, stating:

> This separation of functions is also qualified in three ways. First, before he begins his job, the dispute resolver may talk to advisors and other staff members to obtain background information. Second, with the permission of *all* other parties, he may communicate with decision makers and their advisors about substantive matters. Finally, he may report to decision makers and their advisors on the status of the ADR proceeding at any time, see 18 C.F.R. 385.604(f), provided such discussions do not include any characterizations of the negotiation, including the position being taken by the parties.[17]

This separation of functions guidance lends insight into the relationship between dispute resolvers and agency decision makers and, more importantly, establishes a wall between these functions.

When Is ADR Appropriate?

The availability of a well-designed ADR system that incorporates ethical standards and institutional safeguards does not mean that all cases will or should proceed to ADR. Some cases are not appropriate for ADR and are better served through a traditional process. The 1990 ADR Act provides some guidance on this, stating that ADR is not appropriate when: a definitive or authoritative resolution of the issue is required; the matter involves questions of government policy; a full public record is important; maintaining established policies is important; the matter affects entities who are not parties; and/or the agency must maintain continuing jurisdiction over the matter.[18] This list is not definitive. The key, in this calculation, is to consider the dynamic between the parties and what they hope to achieve. Some helpful questions include:

- Are parties contemplating filing a complaint?
- Do the parties have a history of communication problems?
- Do the parties have the potential for a continuing relationship?
- Is a long-term relationship important to the parties?

- Are there time constraints?
- Do parties appear to be amenable to ADR?
- Might the underlying concerns of the parties be compatible or might they be prioritized differently?
- Do parties misunderstand what is important to the other parties involved?
- Have parties been negotiating for an extended time—but now find themselves at a stalemate?
- Can parties tackle the big issues?
- Do parties wish to maintain control over the outcome of the case?

If the answer to even a few of these questions is "yes," then the case might be appropriate for ADR. What happens at that point is that an agency employee, who is a neutral, such as an independent dispute resolution specialist or mediator, will contact the parties to discuss ADR options. Confidentiality rules apply to this session, which often is called a *convening session;* the neutral cannot discuss the substance of what is said in the convening session with others in their agency other than to say whether or not the parties decide to use ADR. Unless the parties are ordered to ADR by an agency, the ultimate choice of whether to engage in an ADR process rests with the parties. If parties opt to engage in an ADR process, then the agency neutral with whom they initially engaged may become the mediator or facilitator or the parties may select a private neutral.

Steps in a Typical Mediation Process

Assuming the parties accept the option of ADR, what do the next steps look like? The following is an in-depth look at what parties might expect if they opt to pursue mediation, a frequent ADR choice. While each mediator aims to respond to the needs of the parties at the table, there are constants within mediation, including the role of the neutral as a process guide, the parties' control over process and outcome, and the emphasis on confidentiality. The steps in a typical mediation are premediation, mediation session, and follow-up.

The work the mediator does prior to the mediation will set the stage for a productive process. The mediator will schedule a mediation call with attorneys for the parties—or with the parties themselves if they are unrepresented. This call lays the groundwork for the mediation. The mediator will discuss roles and expectations, emphasizing his or her role as a process guide rather than a decision maker. The mediator will also highlight the steps in the process, explaining that parties will likely start out in a joint session during which each party will share their thoughts on the dispute. The mediator will explain that during the mediation, he/she may keep the parties together or elect to talk to each party individually in a separate session called a caucus. The mediator will also talk to the parties about the agreement to mediate that they will sign and the importance of confidentiality. Confidentiality will apply to the parties, who will commit that they will not discuss oral or written communications with anyone not participating in the mediation. Confidentiality also applies to the mediator, who is bound to refrain from disclosing or testifying about what transpired in the mediation. The mediator will also work with the parties to solidify mediation logistics, including when and where the mediation will take place and who will participate. Each party must commit that they will send a decision maker to the mediation—someone who can make commitments at the table to settle the case. During the call, the mediator will also ask the parties to share preliminary information about the dispute. This exchange provides a preview of the issues and can alert the parties if they need to gather more information prior to the mediation session.

During the mediation session, the mediator serves as a process guide. The parties and neutral will sign the agreement to mediate. Next, the mediator opens up the discussion to the parties, giving them an opportunity to share what brought them to the mediation and what they hope to achieve through the process. This is a critical discussion because it informs the direction of the mediation, showcasing the issues that are important to the parties and identifying the priority items that need to be addressed to reach agreement. Throughout the day, the mediator will work with the parties to identify their interests around these issues and to brainstorm and explore potential options for resolution.

If the parties do not reach an agreement during one session (which is often the case in large, multiparty stakeholder efforts), then the mediator will work with the parties to schedule future meeting dates, summarize what has been achieved, and outline what needs to be accomplished to resolve the case. If there are specific tasks that need to be performed, the mediator will ensure that someone is taking ownership of those tasks and that there is a time frame for completing the tasks. This ensures accountability and maintains mediation momentum.

If the parties reach a resolution during the mediation, the mediator will encourage the parties to draft a settlement agreement at that time. Even if the

BOX 9. MULTIPARTY DISPUTE RESOLUTION

A Note about Multiparty Dispute Resolution

Regulatory disputes typically involve multiple parties, requiring dispute resolvers to pay special attention to process management and process dynamics. The mediator must, out of necessity, develop a more formal structure, ensuring that the right parties are at the table and budgeting sufficient time up front so each party has the opportunity to share its perspective. If the representatives at the table are beholden to constituencies, then the mediator needs to work with parties to ensure there is time in the process for representatives to check in with their constituents about the process and come to agreement about the confidentiality implications of doing so. The process of decision-making must also be negotiated with the parties up front. Will the group aim for consensus? Will they opt instead for majority rule? Or will they identify another approach? "The involvement of more than two principals at the negotiation table complicates the situation enormously: social interactions become more complex, information-processing demands increase exponentially, and coalitions can form."[1] The process management and dynamics of multiparty mediations make them especially challenging, but not impossible. To set the stage for agreement, mediators in multiparty disputes must be alert to and plan for the complexities of the parties, the issues, and the process, as was the case with many examples in this book.

1. Leigh Thompson, *The Mind and Heart of the Negotiator*, 4th edition, (London, UK Pearson, 2009), 149.

parties are not ready to finalize settlement language while at the mediation, it is extremely helpful for them to sketch out the key agreement terms in an informal memorandum of understanding or agreement in principle. When the parties finalize the agreement language, the mediator may raise the possibility of including in the final agreement a confidentiality clause if the parties want the agreement to be confidential. The mediator may also talk to the parties about including in the agreement a dispute resolution clause requiring them to return to mediation if there are challenges to implementation or compliance with the agreement and they cannot resolve the dispute on their own.

We are now ready to shift our focus to development and implementation of ADR Programs in the federal and state regulatory realms.

Integrating ADR
into a Regulatory Agency's
Existing Processes

Examining the Application and Integration of ADR at the Federal Energy Regulatory Commission

In part 1, we looked at the regulatory agency context, the ADR context, a dispute resolution design approach to meet the distinct needs in the federal and state regulatory realm, and ADR process integrity. We emphasized that the goal is to supplement, rather than replace, traditional processes. In part 2, we explore the integration of ADR in the federal and state regulatory realm. We do so first through the lens of FERC—an independent federal agency that regulates the transmission and wholesale sales of electricity and natural gas in interstate commerce; regulates the transportation of oil by pipeline in interstate commerce; reviews proposals to build interstate natural gas pipelines, natural gas storage projects, and liquefied natural gas terminals; and issues licenses for nonfederal hydropower projects.[1]

Over the last three decades, FERC has incorporated ADR and collaborative processes into its regulations, rulemakings, and orders, and has taken administrative steps to expand the use of ADR, putting in place discrete process options to resolve disputes, while at the same time integrating ADR techniques and processes throughout the work of the agency. In doing so, FERC demonstrated administrative flexibility and responsiveness, all while meeting its statutory obligations and advancing the public interest.

Table 2 summarizes the range of different ADR processes that FERC uses both before and after a party submits a filing to FERC (pre-filing and post-filing). For the first seven processes—Enforcement Hotline through ADR Tariff Provisions—we describe, in this chapter, how the process works, how it supplements FERC's traditional processes, and how it benefits those involved. Then we discuss FERC's implementation of ADR initiatives in response to the 1990 and 1996 ADR Acts and FERC's changes to its complaint filing requirements to incorporate ADR.

We devote chapters 5, 6, and 7 to examining FERC's independent dispute resolution staff, settlement judges, and trial staff's top sheets—all well-established FERC ADR processes that assist parties to define issues, discuss disagreements, and reach mutually acceptable resolutions. In chapter 8, we shift our attention to ADR use at three state regulatory agencies.

FERC's Hotline/Helpline

FERC makes available the Enforcement Hotline and the Landowner Helpline to provide quick and informal problem-solving and resolution options for FERC stakeholders.

The Enforcement Hotline, which addresses enforcement issues, such as market manipulation, is administered by FERC's Office of Enforcement (OE). Created in 1977 to assist in implementing FERC's regulatory goals, over time OE's focus expanded from ensuring that utility companies comply with their tariff provisions and the Commission's regulations to making sure market participants are not engaging in market manipulation. OE now serves the public interest by protecting consumers through market oversight and surveillance; assuring compliance with tariffs, rules, regulations, and orders; detecting, auditing, and investigating potential violations and crafting appropriate remedies, including civil penalties and other measures.

FERC created the Enforcement Hotline in 1987 to address potential violations of statutes and FERC rules, orders, regulations, license and pipeline conditions, and tariff provisions.[2] Jurisdictional companies and members of the public may ask the Enforcement Hotline for help concerning matters related to FERC jurisdictional issues. The hotline also accepts anonymous calls. Enforcement Hotline calls have included complaints about

- Market manipulation,
- Fraud,
- Bidding anomalies,
- Inappropriate use of financial instruments,
- Fluctuations in available capacity on electric transmission lines and natural gas pipelines,
- Interconnection discrimination,
- Tariff violations, and
- Undue preference to affiliates.

TABLE 2. FERC ADR and Collaborative Process Options

NAME	ADR TECHNIQUE	WHEN USED
Enforcement Hotline	Early Neutral Evaluation	Pre-Filing
Landowners' Helpline	Conciliation Facilitation Mediation	Pre- and Post-Filing
Arbitration	Binding Arbitration	Pre- and Post-Filing
Hydropower Licensing	Collaboration* Facilitation	Pre-Filing
Natural Gas: Pipeline Certificate Collaborative Process and Pipeline Tariff Dispute Resolution	Collaboration Facilitation Mediation Arbitration	Pre-Filing
Oil Pipelines ADR	Arbitration	Post-Filing
Electric: ADR Transmission Tariff Provisions and Permits to Site Interstate Transmission	Mediation Arbitration	Pre- and Post-Filing
Dispute Resolution Service	Conciliation Facilitation Mediation	Pre- and Post-Filing
Settlement Judge	Mediation Early Neutral Evaluation	Post-Filing
Trial Staff Top Sheets	Early Neutral Evaluation	Post-Filing

*Collaboration is a process where stakeholders and the government agency (often) work together to reach a common goal or produce an agreed-to product, such as a report. Collaboration usually happens before parties file with the agency and in advance of disputes developing after a filing is made. The purpose of collaboration is to reach agreement before filing with an agency to avoid a lengthy regulatory process. See https://www.adr.gov/pdf/spectrum_6_23_16_clean.pdf for a spectrum of federal government collaborative processes, prepared by the Collaborative and Facilitative Processes Committee, established by the Interagency ADR Working Group.

The Enforcement Hotline cannot assist in matters related to a formal, docketed filing or contested FERC proceeding (e.g., a complaint) that has been filed or a license application pending before FERC. The goal of the Enforcement Hotline is to address complaints informally, prior to parties filing a formal action, as FERC codified in its procedures in 1999:

> (d) [the] Enforcement Hotline is a forum in which to address quickly and informally any matter within the Commission's jurisdiction concerning natural gas pipelines, electric utilities and hydroelectric projects.[3]

Once a party contacts the Enforcement Hotline, the OE staff conducts an informal investigation of the claim presented. The party may provide written information to the hotline staff to support this effort. For many of the calls, hotline staff advise callers where to find relevant information or direct them to the appropriate FERC office or docketed proceeding. When appropriate, the hotline staff will investigate the facts and provide an informal evaluation of the dispute to the parties, employing the approach and tools of an early neutral evaluation process. This early neutral evaluation sometimes leads to resolution of the caller's concerns. If the complaint or dispute is not resolved through the Enforcement Hotline procedure, the caller may file a formal action with FERC.[4] For fiscal years 2011 to 2016, the Enforcement Hotline received 1,110 calls. The hotline addressed 98 percent of these calls and converted only eight to preliminary investigations. Some of the calls related to matters outside of FERC's jurisdiction or involved matters pending before FERC.[5]

As the focus of the Enforcement Hotline evolved over time, the responsibility for addressing landowner complaints related to natural gas pipeline construction and operation was transferred from the Enforcement Hotline to the Landowner Helpline, administered by the Dispute Resolution Service (DRS), which is discussed in the next chapter.[6]

The Landowner Helpline brings together landowners who have issues or concerns about the pipeline on their land with representatives from the company that constructed or is operating that pipeline. This helpline can also be contacted by any person affected by the construction or operation of a project under the Federal Power Act (FPA). Landowner Helpline staff process requests for information, facilitate resolution of disputes related to land restoration, and respond to other complaints.[7] The staff uses conciliation, facilitation and mediation, as discussed in chapter 1, to assist the parties to resolve their differences.

Arbitration

The Commission has also taken administrative steps to integrate arbitration into the menu of ADR process options. Under Rule 605,[8] parties to a potential arbitration may at any time submit a written proposal to the Commission to use binding arbitration to resolve all or part of any matter in controversy, or anticipated to be in controversy, before FERC. The proposal must be submitted as provided in Rule 604(d),[9] must be in writing, and must contain the information required in

Rule 604(e).[10] FERC may monitor the proceeding and report on the status of the arbitration at any time under Rule 604(f).[11] FERC requires that all parties consent to arbitration before the process starts. Therefore, FERC will give effect to parties' agreements to arbitrate. In *American Municipal Power–Ohio, Inc. v. Dayton Power and Light Co.,*[12] the Commission dismissed a filed complaint, stating:

> We have previously stated that where a filing concerns a dispute that the parties have agreed to arbitrate and where arbitration will not prejudice any party and is not contrary to the public interest, we will generally give effect to the parties' intentions that such dispute be resolved by arbitration.[13]

Parties to an arbitration may request a FERC ALJ or select an arbitrator from outside FERC. Under Rule 605(c),[14] an arbitrator may

- Regulate the course of and conduct arbitral hearings,
- Administer oaths and affirmations,
- Compel the attendance of witnesses and the production of evidence to the extent the Commission is authorized by law to do so, and
- Make awards.

Under Rule 605(d),[15] the arbitrator sets a time and place for the hearing and notifies the participants not less than five days before the hearing. Any participant wishing that there be a record of the proceeding must:

- Prepare the record,
- Notify other participants and the arbitrator of the preparation of the record,
- Furnish copies of the record to all identified participants and the arbitrator, and
- Pay all costs for the record, unless the participants agree otherwise or the arbitrator determines that the costs should be apportioned.

Participants in the arbitration are entitled to be heard, to present evidence material to the controversy, and to cross-examine witnesses at the hearing. To make the process more convenient for the participants, FERC rules allow the arbitrator, with the consent of the participants, to conduct part or all of the hearing by telephone, videoconference, computer, or other electronic means, as long as each participant has an opportunity to participate. The hearing may be conducted expeditiously, and the arbitrator may receive any oral or documentary evidence deemed relevant and exclude any irrelevant, immaterial, unduly repetitious, or privileged evidence. The arbitrator will interpret and apply relevant statutory and regulatory requirements, legal precedents, and policy directives.

To assure fairness, Rule 605(d) prohibits ex parte communications, defined as one party communicating with the arbitrator without the knowledge of the other participant(s), unless the participants agree otherwise.[16] If an ex parte communication occurs, the arbitrator ensures that a memorandum of the communication is prepared and included in the record and that an opportunity for rebuttal is allowed. If the arbitrator receives an ex parte communication, the arbitrator may require the offending participant to show cause as to why the claim of the participant should not be resolved against the participant as a result of the improper conduct.

To assure the arbitrator's decision is timely, FERC rules require the arbitrator to make the award within thirty days after the close of the hearing or the date of the filing of any briefs that the arbitrator authorizes, whichever is later, unless the participants agree otherwise. Under Rule 605(e),[17] the arbitration award must include a discussion of the factual and legal basis for the award. The prevailing participants must file the award with FERC, along with proof of service on all participants. FERC rules also provide:

- The award in an arbitration proceeding will become final thirty days after it is served on all parties.
- A final award is binding on the participants to the arbitration proceeding.
- The award may not be used as precedent or otherwise be considered in any factually unrelated proceeding or in any other arbitration proceeding.[18]

After the 1990 ADR Act was amended in 1996, FERC eliminated from its regulations the earlier provision that provided for FERC review of arbitrators' awards.[19]

Hydropower Licensing

FERC grants licenses to nonfederal hydroelectric plants to operate for a term not exceeding fifty years with certain conditions. The Commission has incorporated ADR tools into hydropower licensing processes. Many multifaceted, complex, and hotly contested environmental and legal issues arise when an applicant is preparing to file a license. On September 21, 2006, FERC issued a *Policy Statement on Hydropower Licensing Settlements* wherein the Commission said that it "looks with great favor on settlements in licensing cases. . . . It can save time and money, avoid the need for protracted litigation, promote the development of positive relationships . . . and give the Commission . . . a clear sense as to the parties' view on the issues presented in each settled case."[20] The Commission further noted its obligations under Section 10(a)(1) of the FPA,[21] as well as the need for evidence to support the application and demonstrate that a settlement is lawful and enforceable, and to address how it meets the comprehensive development criteria and how it provides for recreation as well as other specific measures.[22]

Beginning in 1997, FERC changed the method for applying for and processing license applications by streamlining the traditional licensing process (TLP). The TLP allows for little collaboration or dispute resolution before the applicant files its license application with FERC.[23] After the license applications were filed and protests and interventions were received, the case might be set for hearing before a FERC ALJ. The parties would then conduct discovery and present testimony, followed by filing briefs, an initial decision, and more brief filing before a Commission ruling on the merits of the case. The environmental impact statement was typically prepared before the hearing was ordered and, thus, often became part of the evidentiary record. Often the whole process would take more than five years to complete after the applicant submitted its application to FERC. Under the TLP, settlements were seldom reached—though there were exceptions, as demonstrated in the following example. The two processes that were implemented to correct the challenges of the TLP and enhance the possibility of settlement are the alternative licensing process (ALP) and the integrated licensing process (ILP).

FERC developed the ALP, a pre-filing consultation process that used a more collaborative approach than the TLP. The ALP was designed, in part, to "facilitate greater participation by and improve communication among the potential applicant, resource agencies, Tribes, the public, and Commission staff in a flexible pre-filing consultation process tailored to the circumstances of each case."[24] The goal of the ALP is to resolve environmental disputes before a license application is filed.

In 2004, by Order No. 2002-A, FERC adopted the integrated licensing process (ILP)[25] as an improvement to the ALP, allowing for even more dispute resolution possibilities before filing. The ILP is founded on three fundamental principles: early

BOX 10. FERC TRIAL ATTORNEY FACILITATING AN AGREEMENT

The Kerr Hydroelectric Project

The Kerr Hydroelectric Project (now Seli'š Ksanka Qlispe') is located within the Confederated Tribes of the Salish and Kootenai Reservation (Confederated Tribes) in northwest Montana. In 1930, the FPC issued a fifty-year license to Rocky Mountain Power Company; the license was later transferred to Montana Power Company (MPC). In 1976, MPC and the Confederated Tribes filed competing applications with FERC for a new fifty-year license for the Kerr Project. On July 30, 1983, seven years after the applications were filed, FERC set the competing applications for a hearing before a FERC ALJ. On September 2, 1984, the parties began negotiating, with FERC's assigned trial attorney facilitating the negotiations. On December 5, 1984, a settlement was reached that sought a new license with MPC as the licensee for the first thirty years and the Confederated Tribes as the licensee for the last twenty years of the fifty-year license. On July 17, 1985, FERC approved the settlement.[1] Through this facilitated settlement, the parties met their short- and long-term interests. The Confederated Tribes would be paid higher annual charges for the use of their land for the first thirty years and increased revenue from the sale of the project's energy for the last twenty years. MPC would operate the project as it had for the previous fifty years while recognizing that its role as a utility would change in future years.

All information is public in all the examples in this chapter. One of the authors was the trial staff attorney in this case.

1. 32 FERC ¶ 61,070 (1985), Order Approving Settlement and Issuing License.

issue identification and resolution of the studies needed to fill information gaps and to avoid studies post-filing; integration of other stakeholder-permitting process needs; and established time frames to complete process steps for all stakeholders, including FERC. The ILP is FERC's default process unless FERC approves an applicant's request to use the TLP or ALP.[26]

Under the ILP, the applicant files a notice of intent to file a license application, which includes existing information, a process plan—including a schedule—and a preliminary list of studies and issues. FERC staff prepare a preliminary scoping document with a list of issues, hold meetings with interested parties, and then issue a revised scoping document. All stakeholders submit requests for studies, and the applicant files a proposed study plan. The applicant meets with stakeholders to gather input on the proposed study plan and submits a revised plan to FERC, which FERC reviews and approves, possibly with modifications.

The ILP assures stakeholders that studies will be conducted within a certain time frame. If the parties cannot agree on the studies to be conducted, they have access to an informal dispute resolution process to resolve their differences. In addition, a federal or state agency or Tribe with mandatory conditioning authority may request that a study dispute be referred to a dispute resolution panel. A three-member panel composed of a FERC staff person, the agency or Tribal representative bringing the dispute, and a third person from a preapproved list, who is selected by the other two panelists, makes a recommendation to FERC's Director of the Division of Hydropower Licensing. The Director issues a binding opinion. After study results are available, the applicant submits a preliminary license proposal to FERC. FERC then processes the license application. When the stakeholders agree to the issues and studies and submit information requests before the applicant files, many issues are resolved up front.

In 2005 and again in 2010, FERC staff asked participants using the ILP about ideas, tools, and techniques that were being or could be implemented to achieve the goals of the ILP. Based on that feedback, FERC staff prepared a report, "Ideas for Implementing and Participating in the Integrated Licensing Process (ILP): Tools for Industry, Agencies, Tribes, and Non-Governmental Organizations, Citizens, and FERC Staff (Version 2.0)," to help future ILP participants. The ILP study confirmed that, in most cases, the ILP was achieving its purposes of providing an efficient and effective hydropower licensing process.[27]

The ILP provides an avenue for participants to collaborate up front with each other and the licensee, often through a facilitated process. The process encourages parties to be proactive in finding common ground, far beyond what FERC envisioned years ago with the TLP.

Natural Gas

In October 2000, FERC finalized the rule for Collaborative Procedures for Energy Facility Applications (Order No. 608).[28] Order No. 608 provided an optional procedure for natural gas pipeline applicants to establish and use an alternative, collaborative pre-filing procedure to identify and address issues and disagreements and to resolve those issues before filing. Applicants may adapt the procedures to the circumstances. Other major provisions of Order No. 608 include:

- Applicants notify FERC, the public, including landowners, state and local government officials, and Tribes of their intention to start pre-filing consultations.
- Applicants must develop a pre-filing communications protocol and demonstrate that it made reasonable efforts to contact interested stakeholders. FERC must approve both.
- Once FERC approves applicants' communications protocol and outreach efforts, FERC staff are assigned to facilitate the process.
- Applicants must maintain and make public a file of all relevant documentation.
- Applicants are required to make periodic filings with FERC, summarizing the progress made in the collaborative process.
- When pre-filing discussions result in the applicant reaching agreement with the participants, the applicant submits a settlement agreement along with its application. Parties to such agreements are bound to those agreements after the applicant files.

As with the ALP and ILP, FERC's intent with Order No. 608 was to allow stakeholders to work out agreements in advance of filing and for the applicant to submit a draft environmental assessment or environmental impact statement under the National Environmental Policy Act with its application. The collaborative procedures improve communication, expand public participation, and resolve potential conflicts earlier in the process. Since many issues are resolved before filing, FERC's review and approval would be more expeditious.

In conjunction with Order No. 608, FERC added to its regulations a requirement that potential applicants notify affected landowners about their intent early in the process. This was in direct response to landowners' expressed desire for earlier and better notice of a pipeline's intentions to construct and operate facilities on or near their property. The requirement ensures that landowners are informed in a timely manner and have ample opportunity to participate in FERC's pipeline certificate process.

FERC regulates the rates natural gas pipeline owners charge shippers and the terms and conditions of service. FERC's regulations require that, for affiliate transactions, a natural gas pipeline company must maintain tariff provisions containing procedures used to address and resolve complaints by shippers and potential shippers.[29]

Oil Pipeline ADR

Section 1802(e) of the Energy Policy Act of 1992[30] required FERC to establish ADR procedures to the maximum extent possible in oil pipeline rate proceedings, including requiring negotiation and voluntary arbitration early in contested rate proceedings. In Order No. 561,[31] the Commission established ADR and arbitration procedures for oil pipelines at Section 343.5 of its regulations. The Commission's regulations provide:

> The Commission or other decisional authority may require parties to enter into good faith negotiations to settle oil pipeline rate matters. The Commission will refer all protested rate filings to a settlement judge pursuant to § 385.603 of this chapter for recommended resolution. Failure to participate in such negotiations in good faith is a ground for decision against the party so failing to participate on any issue that is the subject of negotiation by other parties.[32]

Electric

In Order No. 888,[33] FERC required public utilities providing electric transmission services in interstate commerce to file open-access, nondiscriminatory tariffs for such transmission services. The open-access tariffs for new wholesale transactions, new coordination contracts, and energy transactions must conform to the non-rate terms and conditions of FERC's pro forma tariff.

Through Order No. 888, FERC also encouraged the development of independent system operators (ISOs) to operate a state's or region's electricity grid, administer the region's wholesale electricity markets, and provide reliability planning for the region's bulk electricity system, independent of who owned or used the transmission system.

Order No. 888 established eleven principles for the formation of ISOs, with principle No. 11 providing:

An ISO should establish an ADR process to resolve disputes in the first instance. An ISO should provide for a voluntary dispute resolution process that allows parties to resolve technical, financial, and other issues without resort to filing complaints at FERC. We would encourage the ISO to establish rules and procedures to implement alternative dispute resolution processes.[34]

The New England ISO, PJM, New York ISO, Midwest ISO, and California ISO all currently have established dispute resolution processes. Many entities not belonging to an ISO also have dispute resolution processes in their tariffs. The processes typically involve unassisted negotiation and arbitration or unassisted negotiation, mediation, and arbitration.

Under Section 216(b)(1)(C)(i) of the FPA, FERC may issue a permit for the construction of electric transmission facilities in a national corridor if it finds that a state commission or other entity that has authority to approve the siting of the facilities has "withheld approval for more than 1 year after the filing of an application seeking approval pursuant to applicable law or 1 year after the designation of the relevant national interest electric transmission corridor, whichever is later." In its order implementing new regulations under Section 216 of the FPA, FERC stated:

It is incumbent on project sponsors and states to work together to site facilities at the state level, as this would be the most expeditious way to site the facilities. To that end, the Commission will make its Dispute Resolution Service available if parties to a state siting proceeding desire assistance to facilitate the resolution of issues at the state level.[35]

FERC's Application and Integration of ADR-Related Actions

In addition to incorporating ADR tools and processes throughout its work, FERC also implemented ADR regulations to apply the 1990 ADR Act, as well as changes to its complaint procedures. On April 12, 1995, FERC issued Order No. 578[36] to implement the 1990 ADR Act and announced its policy supporting ADR. The provisions of the 1990 ADR Act were, for the most part, codified in Part 385.604 of FERC's regulations (Rule 604).[37] Rule 604 adopted the guidelines for applying ADR techniques and definitions from the 1990 ADR Act and established procedures for submitting, reviewing, and monitoring proposals to use ADR in specific proceedings. Rule 604 provides that participants may, subject to the limitations of paragraph 604(a)(2),[38] use ADR to resolve all or part of any pending matter if the participants agree. Use of ADR by parties is voluntary.[39]

Under Rule 604, ADR refers to any procedure that is used, in lieu of adjudication, to resolve issues in controversy, including but not limited to, settlement negotiations, conciliation, facilitation, mediation, fact finding, minitrials, and arbitration.[40] A neutral may be a permanent or temporary officer or employee of the federal government (including an ALJ) or any other individual who is acceptable to the participants in a dispute resolution proceeding. A neutral must have no official, financial, or personal conflict of interest with respect to the issues in controversy, except that a neutral who is not a government employee may serve if any conflict of interest is disclosed in writing to all participants and all participants agree. A neutral serves at the will of the participants, unless otherwise provided. Neutrals may be selected from among FERC's ALJs, DRS neutrals, other FERC employees, or from rosters kept by the Federal Mediation and Conciliation Service, the Administrative Conference of the United States, or the American Arbitration Association, or from any other appropriate source.

FERC encouraged parties to try the new procedures and stated that they were intended to alleviate the costs and other burdens of regulatory litigation. Parties desiring to initiate dispute resolution procedures may, at any time, submit to the FERC secretary a written proposal, with consent of all the interested parties, to use alternative means of dispute resolution to resolve a matter in controversy before FERC.

FERC recognized the benefits of ADR *when appropriate.* At the same time, in Order No. 578, the Commission observed (as did the 1990 ADR Act) that ADR is not applicable to all disputes. Except as provided in Rule 604(a)(3),[41] the decisional authority cannot consent to the use of an ADR proceeding if

- A definitive or authoritative resolution of the matter is required for precedential value.
- The matter involves or may bear upon policy questions that require additional procedures before a final resolution may be made, and the proceeding would not likely serve to develop a recommended policy.

- Maintaining established policies is of special importance.
- The matter affects persons or organizations that are not parties to the proceeding.
- A full public record of the proceeding is important and a dispute resolution proceeding cannot provide a record.
- The Commission must maintain continuing jurisdiction over the matter, with authority to alter the disposition of the matter in light of changed circumstances, and a dispute resolution proceeding would interfere with the Commission's fulfilling that requirement.[42]

If one or more of the factors outlined in Rule 604(a)(2) is present, ADR may nevertheless be used if the ADR proceeding can be structured to avoid the identified factor or if other concerns outweigh the identified factor. Furthermore, a determination to use or not use a dispute resolution proceeding under Rule 604 is not subject to judicial review.

FERC also took administrative steps to integrate ADR process options into its complaint process. The Commission revised its procedures for handling complaints with Order 602, which encourages and supports the consensual resolution of complaints and recommends ADR as one of the preferred resolution paths.[43] To advance this objective, complainants are required to state whether the parties have used the Enforcement Hotline, FERC's DRS, tariff-based dispute resolution mechanisms, or other informal dispute resolution procedures, and, if not, why; whether the complainant believes that ADR under the Commission's supervision could successfully resolve the complaint; which types of ADR procedures could be used; and whether there is a process on which the parties have agreed for resolving the complaint.[44]

The requirement that complainants consider the use of ADR in their filings is especially important because often there is a lack of understanding of ADR process options and the value in pursuing alternatives to traditional processes, as demonstrated in the following two examples of parties' statements in their complaints:[45]

[The complainant] has attempted for almost a year to resolve this dispute informally. . . . We even sent . . . a settlement proposal. . . . For these reasons, [we] believe that further discussions . . . would not be productive.

[The parties] have already discussed the issues presented without a successful resolution. Consequently, the issues have already been joined through those direct

BOX 11. COMPLAINT CASE EXAMPLE

Phelps Dodge Corp. v. El Paso Natural Gas Co.

In *Phelps Dodge Corp. v. El Paso Natural Gas Co.,* the parties could not resolve matters related to adding a delivery point to provide service to Phelps Dodge's El Paso refinery. At the direction of the Commission, the DRS convened the parties, and the parties agreed to use a mediator from the DRS. In September 1999, the DRS held a one-day mediation session; by the end of the day, an agreement was reached, and further filings with FERC were avoided. With the mediator's assistance, the parties recognized their common business interests and, more importantly, recognized that by working together, they could craft a solution that met each identified interest. Phelps Dodge was able to continue to receive the service it needed. El Paso would transfer a segment of a pipeline that it no longer needed to Southern Union, who would use the pipeline in its gas distribution business. Not only did the settlement close the complaint proceeding, but it also resolved a 1999 filing involving the transfer of facilities that had been the subject of numerous protests.[1]

1. *Phelps Dodge Corporation v. El Paso Natural Gas Company,* 89 FERC ¶ 61,265 (1999).

discussions with little possibility for success of alternative dispute resolution procedures.

Fittingly, Order No. 602 also states that the DRS will work with all those interested in FERC activities to increase awareness and use of ADR.[46] The order adds that parties may use the DRS or the Enforcement Hotline to aid in the informal resolution of disputes before a complaint is filed. Parties may also consider a private mediator before a complaint is filed. Heightened awareness and education help parties understand that ADR may present them with a unique opportunity to meet their interests and the interests of the other side(s) in a creative and mutually beneficial manner.

Conclusion

The processes outlined above reflect that as needs and demands of a regulatory agency and its stakeholders evolve, so too must the processes in place to serve that agency and its stakeholders. More importantly these processes collectively reflect an institutional commitment to and codification of ADR techniques as part of doing business. Further promoting ADR, over the years FERC put in place discrete, ADR-focused units of an independent dispute resolution staff, settlement judges, and trial staff top sheets, discussed in the next chapters.

CHAPTER 5

Appreciating the Role of an Independent Dispute Resolution Staff

Only a few regulatory agencies have a unit dedicated entirely to advancing ADR to address regulatory disputes. For example, the Environmental Protection Agency (EPA) has used ADR to prevent or reduce environmental conflicts and promote constructive collaborative problem solving in various activities and programs. The EPA does so through a separate unit dedicated to this goal—the Conflict Prevention and Resolution Center, housed in the Office of the General Counsel. The center provides environmental ADR services for the EPA, administers agency-wide environmental ADR activities, assists other offices in resolving environmental disputes, and coordinates with a network of ADR staff in EPA's regional offices.

The Federal Maritime Commission (FMC), which regulates and fosters a fair, efficient, and secure maritime transportation system, has an ADR unit, located in the Office of Consumer Affairs and Dispute Resolution Services. The FMC has used ADR to address disputes involving the issuance of licenses and permits, contract awards, shipping, small claims, and tariffs.

The value of an independent ADR unit in a regulatory agency is far-reaching. It reaffirms the separation between agency decision-making units and a neutral dispute resolution unit, which can be important to parties engaged in ADR. It underscores the agency's commitment to ADR, with dedicated staff and funding—as well as the autonomy to do what is needed to institutionalize ADR at the agency. However, creating an independent ADR unit takes time, commitment, and leadership. In this chapter, the founder of and contributors to the Dispute Resolution Service (DRS) at FERC (who are the coauthors) provide an in-depth look at the creation of FERC's independent ADR unit, discussing why the unit was formed, its role and use in addressing regulatory disputes, and steps taken to expand the understanding and use of ADR in the energy regulatory community.

FERC's Dispute Resolution Service

In late 1998, then FERC Chairman James J. Hoecker announced a "Resolve Disputes Initiative" to "promote . . . resolution of contested matters and complaints."[1] The principles of the Resolve Disputes Initiative were to:

- Focus on procedures for more timely resolution of contested matters,
- Augment the use of consensual decision-making by greater reliance on ADR techniques,
- Expand FERC's ADR resources,
- Incorporate ADR as a preferred resolution path for contested proceedings and complaints, and
- Offer opportunities to parties to participate in pre-filing ADR to resolve or narrow issues that would otherwise remain contested after a filing.[2]

In 1999, to foster the Resolve Disputes Initiatives principles, FERC established the DRS, an independent unit dedicated to ADR.[3] The DRS was to be composed of a service-oriented team dedicated to meeting the ADR needs of the parties involved in and impacted by FERC regulation. The DRS had two major functions: to perform ADR services and to promote and enhance the use of ADR before and after parties file disputes at FERC.

The commitment to ADR was reflected in the high-level endorsement and the acknowledgment that the DRS would be positively perceived by those interested in ADR and have: high visibility, an ability to coordinate with all offices, acceptance as an independent and neutral unit, and an ability to commit its time exclusively to ADR duties.

The DRS staff were to serve as neutrals—not involved in the decisional processes, not advocates for positions in contested cases, and not investigators. Discussions between DRS staff and parties were to be kept confidential. More specifically, the DRS staff were to:

- Work closely with other FERC offices to improve ADR awareness and skills by developing and offering education and training on ADR, including conflict avoidance skills and conflict management skills for staff; increasing staff awareness of when ADR might be appropriate; and providing consultation, coaching, and mentoring to staff on ADR use.

- Institutionalize ADR by developing a menu of services and identifying sources of neutrals, identifying cases appropriate for ADR, and developing evaluation criteria for ADR.
- Champion increased use of ADR by engaging in external education efforts on the benefits of ADR and when ADR is appropriate, marketing and advocating increased use of ADR to external participants, publicizing the successful use of ADR in all Commission areas, and conducting outreach programs.
- Work with parties to identify the most appropriate ADR process for their dispute by conducting convening sessions with parties to explain the ADR process options and to identify the most appropriate option for their dispute and educating participants on what to expect in an ADR process.

In 1999, FERC's Dispute Resolution Specialist, as defined in section 3(b) of the 1990 ADR Act, was also appointed as the Director of the DRS. In that role, the Director represented FERC with other organizations and fostered cooperative relationships with federal and state agencies on ADR matters. The Director was also charged with providing leadership and vision in designing and implementing a program that promoted and resolved disputes through the use of consensual processes.

DRS Case Management

There are multiple avenues by which parties come to FERC's DRS. Often parties seek out the DRS, contacting the DRS for a confidential session to explore ADR options before making a filing. The DRS staff may contact parties to explain ADR process options and inquire whether they are interested in dispute resolution. Whatever path the parties take to ADR, the DRS staff member who convenes the parties serves as a neutral in the proceeding and, therefore, is subject to all relevant ethical requirements. Pursuant to the separation of functions rule, DRS staff are prohibited from participating in or providing advice on contested matters pending before FERC.

The DRS representative convening the parties acts as a guide and helps the parties understand the different processes available. Throughout the convening process, DRS staff answer the parties' questions and underscore that the parties do not compromise the status of their cases by exploring alternative settlement options. Convening does not delay FERC's ordinary processing of a case unless the

BOX 12. MULTIPARTY PIPELINE OPERATIONAL DISPUTE

Operational Balancing Agreements

FERC adopted a regulation requiring each interstate pipeline to enter into an Operational Balancing Agreement (OBA) at all points of interconnection between its system and the system of another interstate or intrastate pipeline. In one case, several pipelines had unresolved differences regarding OBAs and their form. The DRS was asked by the Director of the Office of Pipeline Regulation to convene a session with these pipelines and the entities that interconnected with them. For two months, the DRS worked with the parties. As a result of the facilitative efforts, most of the over forty OBAs at issue were resolved.

All information is public in all the examples in this chapter. The authors of this book served as the third party neutral in each example in this chapter.

parties request FERC hold the case in abeyance while the ADR process goes forward; nor will a convening session bind the parties to continue with an ADR process. Parties do not give up any procedural rights by participating in an ADR process.

Once the parties select a process—most typically a mediation process—a neutral is selected. The parties may select a DRS representative or an ALJ as a third-party neutral or select a neutral from outside FERC. The process informs the role the third-party neutral will play. The DRS representative typically plays a facilitative role, working with parties to move away from their positions and think about how they can work together to obtain their short- and long-term interests. If the parties opt for a more evaluative approach, they may choose a settlement judge or a subject-matter expert neutral to conduct an early neutral evaluation. The results of the early neutral evaluation will inform the parties how to proceed.

Parties are not alone in seeking the services of DRS. Sometimes other entities within, or even outside of, the Commission have a role in steering a case into ADR. A request may come from another office within the Commission, as detailed in the Operational Balancing Agreements example. And sometimes, cases take a more circuitous route to get to the DRS, as detailed in the Supreme Court remand example.

The various pathways by which cases come to the DRS underscore that the office quickly became an integral part of the work of the Commission, offering alternatives to traditional processes when appropriate and needed.

BOX 13. SUPREME COURT REMAND—NEVER TOO LATE TO GIVE MEDIATION A TRY

Western Energy Crisis

This case ended up in DRS after a circuitous procedural history. The *Western Energy Crisis* originated from the 2000s energy crisis. Between December 2001 and February 2002, NV Energy, Golden State, and Public Utility District No. 1 of Snohomish County filed complaints seeking to abrogate or reform their bilateral wholesale contracts. The Commission held a hearing on the complaints to address several issues, including whether the dysfunctional California spot markets adversely affected the long-term bilateral markets and, if so, whether modification of any individual contract at issue was warranted; whether the *Mobile-Sierra* public interest standard of review or the ordinary just and reasonable standard of review should be applied; what the effect of the contracts was on the financial health of the purchasers; and whether the contract modification had an impact on national energy markets.[1]

On June 26, 2008, the Supreme Court, after review of the Ninth Circuit's decision,[2] remanded the case to FERC to amplify or clarify its findings on whether the contracts at issue had imposed an excessive burden on consumers "down the line" and whether any of the sellers in the case had engaged in unlawful activities in the spot markets that affected any of its contracts at issue in the case. On December 18, 2008, the Commission issued an Order on Remand, pursuant to the Supreme Court's remand instructions, which established hearing procedures but held the hearings in abeyance to allow time to conduct settlement discussions with a settlement judge or DRS.[3] The parties opted to proceed with DRS's help.

By February 2011, the DRS had concluded the final mediation in the five cases remanded to the Commission by the US Supreme Court: *Snohomish v. Morgan Stanley, Golden State Water Co. v. Mirant American Energy Marketers, NV Energy v. Allegheny Energy Supply Company, NV Energy v. AEP,* and *NV Energy v. BP Energy.* With DRS mediator assistance, parties resolved their disputes over appropriate refund amounts through consensual agreement, finally allowing the parties to put this litigation and the potential for more appeals behind them.

1. *Nevada Power Company and Sierra Pacific Power Company v. Enron Power Marketing, Inc., et al,* 125 FERC ¶ 61,312 (2008).
2. *Pub. Util. Dist. No. 1 of Snohomish County v. FERC,* 471 F.3d 1053 (9th Cir. 2006).
3. *Nevada Power Co., et. al.,* 125 FERC ¶ 61,312 (2008).

DRS Efforts to Promote and Enhance the Use of ADR

In conjunction with establishing avenues through which parties could avail themselves of ADR, the DRS also conducted internal and external outreach to champion ADR as a potential first choice in dispute resolution. Internally, the DRS educated FERC staff on the benefits of ADR and provided formal training classes in facilitation, negotiation, and strategies for dealing with difficult people and difficult conversations. Externally, the DRS met with groups to explain ADR. DRS also provided formal training to other regulatory agencies and groups, such as the California Public Utilities Commission, New York Public Service Commission, Michigan State University Institute of Public Utilities, Veterans Administration, Department of Interior, Surface Transportation Board, and Nuclear Regulatory Commission.

The goal of the outreach efforts was multifold. Internally, the outreach was designed to raise awareness of ADR processes and skills that might assist FERC offices in their work with the regulated community and, on occasion, provide an alternative path to resolve contested issues. Externally, the outreach was designed to spread the word to FERC's regulated community about the availability and applicability of ADR process options. The outreach was also designed to disseminate information to other communities where alternative options to resolve disputes might prove beneficial and to support other federal and state agencies' in their efforts to institutionalize ADR process options.

DRS Results

From the outset, the DRS tracked its results. Evaluative tools, such as a post-ADR process or post-training survey, captured the impact of ADR and reaffirmed the value of a robust ADR effort at a regulatory agency. For example, in the first ten years of its existence, the DRS received more than five hundred requests and referrals for energy and environmental cases, facilitated over 350 outreach events, and guided parties through 227 dispute resolution processes. Settlement rates for ADR processes during this time hovered close to 86 percent. Pipeline cases proved especially successful, with an average settlement rate of 90 percent.

In addition to the DRS-led efforts to track results, FERC also engaged the Harvard Negotiation and Mediation Clinical Program to gather input from parties who had engaged in FERC-led ADR processes. The parties were polled on their experiences, perspectives, and suggestions for fortifying the program. The resulting overview, "Alternative Dispute Resolution in the Federal Government: What's Up at the Federal Energy Regulatory Commission and Elsewhere," reported satisfaction with DRS services and the professionalism and skill of the DRS staff. Parties suggested expanding the use of ADR earlier in FERC projects and proceedings, especially in pre-filing processes.

A Model Approach

The development and integration of the FERC DRS provides an example of a dispute systems design approach that captured the voices of those who would utilize ADR services, capitalized on the wave of ADR momentum, incorporated creative ideas, and fostered collaboration with internal and external partners. Most importantly, FERC DRS staff were empowered to create a meaningful, sustainable program. Leadership was critical to this effort, devoting resources to staff development, encouraging staff autonomy to be flexible in ADR process options, supporting training and outreach, and incorporating tracking and evaluation to provide quantifiable feedback on the value of ADR. The ADR regulations served to memorialize the intent to integrate ADR into Commission processes. And, although each regulatory agency is different, the FERC approach provides a model for other regulatory agencies and for the private sector to reference when developing or fortifying their own ADR Programs. In the realm of ADR, one size does not fit all, but understanding what has worked in one area can inspire ideas and momentum to integrate ADR into other areas.

Case Examples Showing the Range of Issues DRS Mediated

DRS staff mediated cases with a range of issues. From the integration of a utility into an ISO to complicated tax issues, the DRS was positioned to quickly respond to case requests, at any point in the life cycle of a case at FERC.

BOX 14. INTEGRATION OF UTILITY INTO AN ISO

Integration of Utility into an ISO: MEAN, MMTG, MISO, and MidAmerican

On June 1, 2009, the Midwest Independent Transmission Operator, Inc. (MISO) and MidAmerican Energy Company (MidAmerican) proposed revisions to MISO's Open Access tariff to facilitate the integration of MidAmerican into MISO as a transmission-owning member. The Midwest Municipal Transmission Group (MMTG) and the Municipal Energy Agency of Nebraska (MEAN) filed with FERC opposing MidAmerican's joining MISO. MMTG and MEAN, whose operations depended on using MidAmerican's transmission system, complained that their transmission costs would rise because the MISO transmission allocation system did not allocate them sufficient transmission rights to serve their native load, thereby requiring them to buy more rights, which would increase the costs to their customers. MMTG and MEAN argued this violated the terms of an existing agreement with MidAmerican.

FERC's DRS representative assisted the parties to explain their issues and to understand what was important to each party. Once the parties understood the complex MISO transmission allocation rules and the MMTG and MEAN needs, they were able to discuss options to satisfy all parties' interests. On January 7, 2011, MISO, MMTG, and MEAN filed a joint request to approve a partial settlement and a request by MMTG and MEAN to hold the proceedings in abeyance to permit further negotiations. After further mediated sessions, MMTG, MEAN, MidAmerican, and MISO reached a settlement that resolved all disputes among the parties regarding MidAmerican's integration into MISO, clarified previously disputed issues, and better protected MMTG and MEAN with respect to certain congestion cost hedging consistent with MISO's Open Access Tariff.[1]

1. *Midwest Independent Transmission System Operator, Inc.*, 138 FERC ¶ 61,214 (2012).

BOX 15. DELIVERY CANCELLATION DISPUTE

Phillips Pipeline and Silver Eagle

On May 16, 2001, Phillips Pipeline Company (Phillips) filed to cancel delivery of crude petroleum to a refinery owned by Silver Eagle Refining Woods Cross Plant (Silver Eagle), who opposed and protested the request. Thirty days later, FERC directed the

Director of the DRS to convene the parties to identify a process that would foster negotiation and agreement.[1] Seven days later, the Director of DRS conducted a successful mediation session with the parties. On June 25, 2001, a settlement was filed to resolve all issues in the proceeding. On July 6, 2001, FERC approved the settlement.[2] The total time from the filing to FERC approval was fifty-one days.

1. *Phillips Pipe Line Company,* Order Accepting and Suspending Tariff and Referring Proceeding to Dispute Resolution Service, 95 FERC ¶ 61,416 (2001).
2. *Phillips Pipe Line Company,* 96 FERC ¶ 61,030 (2001).

BOX 16. TRANSMISSION SCHEDULING PRACTICES AND RELIABILITY

BPA and Amp Parties

This technically complex case raised contractual questions dating back to 1963 and involved North American Reliability Corporation (NERC) standards, Bonneville Power Administration's (BPA) Hot Springs substation, and a 230 kV transmission line subject to an agreement by four utilities. The 230 kV transmission facilities (known as the Amps Line) extend generally from the border of Wyoming, north through Idaho, terminating at Noxon, Montana. In 1965, the predecessors of the current owners of the 230 kV transmission facilities (Avista Corporation, Idaho Power Company, NorthWestern Corporation, and PacifiCorp, collectively known as the Amp parties) entered into an Interconnection Agreement. BPA operates the Hot Springs substation that interconnects with the Amps Line in Montana. The Amps Line and the Hot Springs substation are part of the facilities that comprise the Montana-to-Northwest transmission path.

NorthWestern Corporation is the balancing authority under NERC and was responsible for scheduling and monitoring transmission on the Amps Line. When NorthWestern (in compliance with mandatory NERC reliability standards) notified customers of its proposal regarding e-Tags, parties objected to NorthWestern's actions. (E-Tags are requests to schedule electric interchange transactions to flow into, out of, or within certain areas.)[1] The parties entered into discussions, and confusion arose regarding scheduling practices at Hot Springs related to facility ownership, metering boundaries, bilateral and multiparty agreements, and past scheduling practices.

After the parties failed to arrive at a solution, they agreed to mediation conducted by FERC's DRS.

All parties reached an agreement, entitled the Capacity Management Procedures Agreement, which was filed with FERC. By letter dated June 15, 2009, the agreement was accepted for filing by FERC.[2] Without a settlement, litigation would have been lengthy and complicated, addressing the application of contracts entered into in the 1960s and later. The arguments would have focused on what rights each party had without consideration of how the facilities could be best utilized. With mediation, the parties, and specifically the technical experts, were able to better understand steps that could not only meet the parties' interests but also improve on the use of the facilities while the negotiations took place, and enable NorthWestern to meet its obligations under NERC.

1. See, 141 FERC ¶ 61,235, 18 C.F.R. Part 366, [Docket No. RM11-12-000; Order No. 771] Availability of E-Tag Information to Commission Staff (Issued December 20, 2012), specifically page 1 footnote 2 of the Final Rule for the definition of e-Tag.

2. See Docket No. ER09-1023-000, Letter Order June 15, 2009.

BOX 17. COMPLEX FINANCIAL ISSUE

Cedar Bay and PG&E

By order issued on December 21, 1993, FERC recertified the facility of Cedar Bay Generating Company, LP, as a qualifying facility (QF).[1] FERC required that a true-up be performed on the disposition of the interest in the QF to ensure that PG&E did not receive more than 50 percent of the stream of benefits in connection with its involvement in the QF. On September 7, 2004, Cedar II Power Corporation (Cedar II) filed a petition for a declaratory order to determine the amount of a true-up obligation owed indirectly by PG&E affiliate—National Energy & Gas Transmission (NEGT) and Raptor Holding Company (Raptor)—under the 1993 Order. Cedar II's petition contended that the emergence from bankruptcy of NEGT triggered a true-up payment obligation that was required by the order recertifying the project as a QF. Cedar II was concerned that if no true-up payment was made, electric utilities would receive more than 50 percent of the stream of benefits and its QF designation would be jeopardized.

On July 3, 2003, NEGT declared bankruptcy. The bankruptcy court approved NEGT's plan of reorganization that provided for the elimination of PG&E's equity interest in NEGT and the issuance of new debt and equity securities to the new owners of NEGT. NEGT's bankruptcy plan was expected to become effective in October 2004. NEGT, Raptor, and the Unsecured Creditors of NEGT filed petitions to intervene. BNP Paribas, New York Branch, in its capacity as agent for certain lenders, also intervened.

After the filing of the interventions, FERC's DRS conducted a one-day mediation session that led to a settlement filed on September 7, 2004. By order issued on September 30, 2004, FERC approved the settlement, finding that the settlement benefitted customers because it resolved the amount of true-up payment required and ensured that the project would retain its QF status.[2]

1. *Cedar Bay Generating Company, Limited Partnership*, 65 FERC ¶ 62,232 (1993). For a description of a qualifying facility, see "What is a Qualifying Facility?" FERC website, https://www.ferc.gov/industries/electric/gen-info/qual-fac/what-is.asp.

2. *Cedar II Power Corporation*, 108 FERC ¶ 61,322 (2004).

BOX 18. AN ALTERNATIVE LICENSING PROCESS—MEDIATION

The Upper River Hydroelectric Project

On July 7, 2005, the Sacramento Municipal Utility District (SMUD) filed an application for a new license for its Upper American River Hydroelectric Project (Upper American Project)[1] and to construct the proposed Iowa Hill Pumped Storage Development (Iowa Hill Development). Prior to its filing and under the auspices of an Alternative Licensing Process, SMUD in 2001 initiated consultation with state and federal resource agencies, local governments, nongovernmental organizations, and members of the public to identify issues and to design and conduct studies in 2003 and 2004. Following the submission of the license application, SMUD and the interested parties, with the assistance of a mediator from FERC's DRS, continued to negotiate over conditions to be included in a new license. On February 1, 2007, SMUD filed a comprehensive settlement agreement related to relicensing the Upper American Project.[2] The settlement was signed by fifteen stakeholders and resolved all issues among the signatories related to the relicensing.[3]

FERC staff issued a final environmental impact statement on March 14, 2008. On July 23, 2014, FERC issued a new license that incorporated forty-four of the settlement's proposed articles that related to environmental resources.[4] As to why the license was not issued for seven years after the settlement was filed, FERC had to wait until October 4, 2013, when the California Water Board issued the required water quality certificate, which included twenty-seven project-specific conditions that were found to be consistent with the settlement. This case demonstrates that, when parties collaborate, many of their interests are met more quickly through a settlement process than through a judicial process.

1. The project consists of seven developments located on the Rubicon River, Silver Creek and South Fork American River in El Dorado and Sacramento Counties in California. The project is also located on lands within a national forest and on lands administered by the U.S. Bureau of Land Management (BLM).

2. The settlement also addressed an agreement reached on Pacific Gas and Electric Company (PG&E)'s Chili Bar Hydroelectric Project, which is located below SMUD's project.

3. Signators to the settlement were American Whitewater, American River Recreation Association, US Bureau of Land Management, California Department of Parks and Recreation, California Department of Fish and Game, California Outdoors, California Sportfishing Protection Alliance, Camp Lotus, Foothill Conservancy, US Forest Service, Friends of the River, US Department of Interior, US National Park Service, PG&E, Rich Platt, Hilde Schweitzer, Theresa Simsiman, and SMUD.

4. *Sacramento Municipal Utility District*, 148 FERC ¶ 62,070 (2014).

CHAPTER 6

Resolving Cases with the FERC Settlement Judge Process

Settlement judges are FERC Administrative Law Judges (ALJs) who promote and encourage settlement negotiations as a means to expeditiously resolve cases. The ALJ role has evolved through the years. Before 1946, regulatory agencies assigned staff members to serve as "hearing" or "trial" examiners in proceedings requiring the taking of evidence. The Interstate Commerce Commission and the Federal Trade Commission were early users of hearing examiners in the federal government.[1] The Federal Power Commission (FPC),[2] the precursor to FERC, also utilized this role early on, as evidenced by the November 3, 1939, "Order Authorizing Commissioners and Others to Preside at Hearings." The order found that "[given the] complexity and extent of such duties and responsibilities necessary to the efficient and prompt performance thereof . . . trial examiners and other members of the Commission's staff, as well as members of the Commission, [should] be authorized to hold public hearings, including administering oaths, and [taking] evidence."[3]

With the passage of the Administrative Procedure Act (APA) in 1946,[4] Congress sought to ensure fairness and due process in all agency actions and proceedings involving rulemakings and adjudications. The APA sought to achieve uniformity between the many government agencies by establishing general standards for how agencies should act. The APA also created the position of "hearing examiners" and included protections to preserve the independence of these hearing officers.

In 1967, John W. Macy Jr., former Chair of the US Civil Service Commission, observed:

> Hearing examiners appointed under the Act conduct hearings . . . [and] make decisions . . . that have far-reaching impact on individual rights and property . . . they hold key positions in agencies whose responsibilities, in the words of President

Kennedy, "permeate every sphere and almost every activity in our national life [and] have a profound effect upon the direction and pace of our economic growth"; and they play this critical role in a maelstrom of competing private and public interests.[5]

In 1978, Congress changed the title "hearing examiners" to "administrative law judges." Today, ALJs are located in over twenty-five federal agencies, addressing issues relating to licensing, just and reasonable rates, tariffs, discrimination, airline routes, unfair labor practices, mergers, and securities. In *Butz v. Economou,* the US Supreme Court observed that the role of a modern federal ALJ may be compared with that of a trial judge, stating:

> There can be little doubt that the role of the modern federal hearing examiner or administrative law judge within this framework is "functionally comparable" to that of a judge. His powers are often, if not generally, comparable to those of a trial judge: he may issue subpoenas, rule on proffers of evidence, regulate the course of the hearing, and make or recommend decisions. See 556 (c). More importantly, the process of agency adjudication is currently structured so as to assure that the hearing examiner exercises his independent judgment on the evidence before him, free from pressures by the parties or other officials within the agency.[6]

FERC's Settlement Judge Program

In 1946, Congress recognized the role of settlements in the administrative process. Section 554(c) of the APA provides in pertinent part:

> (c) The agency shall give interested parties opportunity for—
> (1) *the submission and consideration of* facts, arguments, *offers of settlement,* or proposals of adjustment when time, the nature of the proceeding, and the public interest permit; and
> (2) to the extent the parties are unable to determine a controversy by consent, hearing and decision on notice and in accordance with section 556 and 557 of this title.[7]

FERC was a forerunner among federal agencies in promoting and encouraging the settlement process, with the value of this role recognized over forty years ago.

As recounted by former FERC Deputy Chief ALJ William J. Cowan and Sandra Barbulescu, Law Clerk, in their paper titled "Settlement Judge Process at the Federal Energy Regulatory Commission":

> The usefulness of providing a trained and respected neutral to assist in reaching settlements of the FERC's most complex and difficult cases became apparent in 1977, during the rehearing of a case involving natural gas curtailment issues on the Southern Natural Gas Company System. The State of Georgia, a party to the case, suggested that the Commission use the Administrative Law Judge who had presided at the hearings, Chief Administrative Law Judge Curtis L. Wagner, Jr., to lead structured settlement discussions. Those settlement discussions concluded successfully and an agreement to resolve the issues in the case was presented to and approved by the Commission. The FERC Chairman at that time, Charles B. Curtis, concluded that the agency would benefit from a codification of a settlement process conducted under the direction of an agency Administrative Law Judge and he initiated a rule that would formalize a settlement judge process. (pp. 3–4; footnotes omitted)[8]

On October 3, 1979, the Commission proposed to incorporate into its Rules of Practice and Procedure the practice of using an ALJ as a settlement judge. By Order No. 90,[9] issued in 1980, Rule 1.18 was amended to provide for procedures for the appointment of a settlement judge. In 1982, Rule 1.18 was re-designated as 18 C.F.R. § 385.603.[10] (Rule 603)

> At FERC, a settlement judge is an ALJ trained in ADR techniques and authorized to work with the parties and to assist them in resolving a dispute without the need for a formal administrative hearing. The settlement judge process is an adjunct to other traditional methods used by ALJs to promote settlements such as pre-hearing conferences. Settlement judge proceedings require the participation of the parties. The settlement judge is prohibited from discussing the case with the presiding judge. Statements and conduct of the parties at settlement negotiations before the settlement judge are not admissible in later proceedings before the Commission.

Pursuant to Rule 603,[11] there are different avenues to appoint a settlement judge:

- Rule 603(c)[12] allows any participant to request the appointment of a settlement judge with the presiding officer, or, if there is no presiding officer for the proceeding, with the Commission. A presiding officer may also request the Chief ALJ to appoint a settlement judge.

- Rule 603(d)[13] provides that the Commission may also order the appointment of a settlement judge.
- Rule 603(e)[14] provides that the Chief ALJ may appoint a settlement judge for any proceeding, if requested by the presiding officer under paragraph (c)(2) of this section or if the presiding officer concurs in a motion made under paragraph (c)(1) of this section.
- Rule 603(f)[15] provides that the Chief ALJ will appoint a settlement judge by an order, which specifies whether and to what extent the proceeding is suspended, pending termination of settlement negotiations conducted in accordance with this section. The order may confine the scope of any settlement negotiations to specified issues.

On June 9, 1998, the Chief ALJ issued a notice providing that once settlement procedures are instituted, participants may let the Chief ALJ know which ALJ they prefer. If the requested judge is available, the Chief ALJ would designate that ALJ as the settlement judge. If the requested judge was unavailable, the participants would be informed and given an opportunity to select another judge if they so desired. If the participants had no preference, the Chief ALJ would select a settlement judge for the case. Recently, FERC's Office of Administrative Law Judges moved to a model of looking at workflows before assigning a settlement judge to promote rotational assignment of cases.

Settlement judge proceedings invite the participation of the parties. However, the judge controls the process. The settlement judge convenes and presides over conferences and settlement negotiations between the parties and assesses the practicalities of a potential settlement. The settlement judge is obligated to report to the Chief ALJ the status of the settlement negotiations, not later than thirty days after appointment. The settlement judge may recommend termination or continuation of settlement negotiations. Periodic status reports are also the norm while settlement negotiations continue.[16]

As previously noted, the Commission's settlement judges are ALJs trained in ADR techniques. Authorized to facilitate negotiations with the parties, settlement judges can employ any of the several ADR applications. The settlement judge may be evaluative when addressing the issues. In order to encourage free flow of information, the settlement judge is prohibited from discussing the case with an agency decision maker or with advisory staff.

Uncontested settlements can be certified to the Commission by the presiding settlement judge under Rule 602(g).[17] In general, a settlement offer must include a separate explanatory statement and copies of or references to every document, testimony, and exhibit, including record citations (if there is a record), relevant to the settlement offer. The offer must be served on all parties. Comments on the settlement are permitted, and failure to file a comment constitutes a waiver of all objections to the settlement offer.[18] Any comment that contests a settlement offer by alleging a dispute as to a genuine issue of material fact must include an affidavit detailing the issue by specific reference to documents, testimony, or other items included in the settlement offer, or by items not included in the settlement that are relevant to support the claim. Reply comments may include responding affidavits.[19]

If a settlement offer is uncontested, the settlement judge will certify it to the Commission, along with any comments. An uncontested offer may be approved by the Commission upon a finding that the settlement appears to be fair and reasonable and in the public interest.[20] If the settlement judge determines that the offer is contested, in whole or in part, by any participant, s/he may certify all or part of the offer to the Commission but only if paragraph (h)(2)(ii) or (iii) of Rule 602 applies.[21]

A settlement offer that is not approved by the Commission and any comment on that offer will not be admissible in evidence against any participant who objects to its admission. Any discussion of the parties with respect to a settlement offer that is not approved by the Commission is not subject to discovery or admissible in evidence.[22]

Selected Examples of Successful Settlement Judge Proceedings

The use of settlement judges at FERC has increased dramatically. In fiscal years 1990 and 1991, there were seventeen settlement judge proceedings, whereas for fiscal years 2000 and 2001 there were eighty-eight settlement judge proceedings. The use of the settlement judge process at FERC remains high.

The two examples of the settlement judge process illustrate an early successful application of the settlement judge process and a recent success in a complicated,

BOX 19. SUCCESSFUL APPLICATION OF THE SETTLEMENT JUDGE PROCESS: TWO EXAMPLES

Northeast U.S. Pipeline Projects

In Northeast U.S. Pipeline Projects, the Chief ALJ was appointed to eliminate some of the competitive issues, utilize and improve previous proposals, and separate mutually exclusive projects and markets.[1] Over the six months that followed, the Chief Judge held ninety-six conferences and meetings with individual parties. A total of thirty-seven applications involving thirteen projects were settled.[2]

TAPS

On December 15, 2017, a settlement offer was filed by numerous parties in a case that was the product of extensive settlement negotiations presided over by a senior ALJ acting as settlement judge. The settlement resolved forty-six pending Commission dockets and a decade of TAPS litigation, captured a total savings of one billion dollars (as calculated by FERC's trial staff), provided for the withdrawal of petitions for review with the US Court of Appeals for the District of Columbia Circuit, and provided hundreds of millions of dollars of refunds to Alaska.[3]

All information is public in all the examples in this chapter.

1. *Northeast U.S. Pipelines Projects*, 44 FERC ¶ 61,150 (1998).
2. *Northeast U.S. Pipelines Projects*, 46 FERC ¶ 61,012. (1989).
3. See letter of offer of settlement filed by BP Pipelines (Alaska) Inc., Docket No. IS09-348-000 and 45 other dockets. See also the trial staff's comments filed January 4, 2018.

BOX 20. MULTIPARTY TWO-STAGE MEDIATION

Duquesne Light, PJM, and MISO

On November 8, 2007, Duquesne Light Company (Duquesne) filed a petition with FERC requesting that FERC approve its conditional request to withdraw from PJM Interconnection, LLC (PJM), to join the Midwest ISO (MISO). Thirty-six petitions to intervene raised complex issues. Resolution of the issues consisted of two phases. On January 17, 2008, FERC conditionally approved the request and required Duquesne to address certain issues that were not sufficiently addressed.[1]

While Duquesne and the parties continued submitting pleadings at FERC regarding Duquesne's 2007 petition, and after Duquesne and the MISO made an integration filing with FERC, the DRS mediated settlement negotiations between the parties. On December 12, 2008, Duquesne, PJM, and fifteen other parties filed a settlement agreement, in which Duquesne sought to withdraw from the Commission's consideration its request to withdraw from PJM. MISO objected to the settlement, arguing that Duquesne was contractually committed to remain a member of MISO for five years and requesting an exit fee for Duquesne's premature withdrawal. On January 29, 2009, FERC accepted the settlement, stating that MISO and other affected parties may make a separate filing in a new proceeding to raise its issues or may pursue these issues in an appropriate judicial forum.[2] MISO subsequently filed an action in District Court, alleging breach of contract. Duquesne argued that the case should be referred to FERC under the primary jurisdiction doctrine.

On August 10, 2010, the District Court ordered MISO to seek the Commission's opinion on two issues.[3] MISO filed a motion with FERC in response to the District Court's directive. FERC ordered the filing of initial and reply briefs on the issues. On February 16, 2012, FERC found that Duquesne's agreement with MISO created a binding commitment. FERC ordered a hearing and settlement judge proceedings on what a just and reasonable exit fee should be.[4] On September 5, 2012, the settlement judge certified an uncontested settlement that provided for a two-million-dollar exit fee.[5] On December 31, 2012, FERC approved the settlement.[6]

One of the authors of this book served as the mediator in this case.
1. *Duquesne Light Company,* 122 FERC ¶ 61,039 (2008).
2. *Duquesne Light Company.* 126 FERC ¶ 61,074, *reh'g denied,* 127 FERC ¶ 61,186 (2009).
3. *Midwest Indep. Transmission Sys. Operator v. Duquesne Light Co.,* No. 1:09-dv-TWP-DML at 8 (S.D. Ind. Jul. 12, 2010).
4. *Duquesne Light Company,* 138 FERC ¶ 61,111 (2012).
5. *Duquesne Light Company,* 140 FERC ¶ 63,018 (2012).
6. *Duquesne Light Company,* 141 FERC ¶ 61,278 (2012).

contested case. The example of a multiparty two-stage mediation illustrates a successful resolution using multiple ADR options—a DRS mediator and a settlement judge.

As evidenced here, the settlement judge option provides yet another avenue for parties to pursue resolution at FERC. The numbers suggest that many parties avail themselves of this option. But if they do not, they will, nonetheless, be well informed about other avenues for pursuing resolution. By notice issued on July 21, 2000, the Chief ALJ announced new ADR procedures for initial prehearing conferences. At all subsequent initial prehearing conferences, the presiding judge will, at some point, advise the parties of available ADR procedures and take a recess in order for the parties and the Commission trial staff to explore, privately and off-the-record, the desirability of using one of the available ADR procedures. The parties are required to be prepared to discuss the desirability of ADR procedures in the proceeding and the available types of ADR. This process, now memorialized as part of the prehearing conference, is yet one more example of the institutionalization of ADR at FERC.

CHAPTER 7

Looking at the Role of Independent Trial Staff in the Settlement Process

DRS staff and settlement judges play a clearly-defined role—as neutrals—in facilitating resolution of contested matters at FERC. Trial staff at FERC are not neutral, yet they too play an integral role in achieving settlements.

At many federal agencies, independent agency trial staff participate in hearings before ALJs. Former Federal Power Commission (FPC) Chief Judge Joseph Zwerdling described this important and distinct role that agency trial staff play in hearings:

> At agencies, such as the Federal Power Commission and the Civil Aeronautics Board, the staff participates fully as a party in every proceeding . . . [with the] objective . . . to present positions which it believes to be in the public interest . . . The staff's objective is also to insure that a full and adequate record is made, providing an accurate and complete picture, which will be of maximum help to the hearing examiner and to the Commission. The interplay between the conflicting parties and the staff in open hearing, each having a different role to perform, produces useful and desirable results.[1]

Trial staff have played an important role at FERC and its predecessor, the FPC, since the early 1930s.[2] As noted, trial staff are not neutrals, but rather advocates for a client—and that client is the public interest. As former Chief Judge Zwerdling noted in 1973:

> There is, of course, no doubt that the staff, as a matter of general principle, desires to serve the public interest as distinguished from the narrower private interests of the parties. The staff is just as much interested in serving its client, the public interest, as each private practitioner is interested in serving his client.[3]

As nondecisional employees, trial staff are not constrained by ex parte rules and are free to facilitate settlement by meeting separately with individual parties or groups of parties. Trial staff are also bound by the separation of functions rule, which prohibits them from discussing the case and all nonpublic communications made during a settlement conference with other parts of FERC. This is critical to the integrity of the trial staff role.

Also critical to the integrity and reputability of the role is the expertise of trial staff. For trial staff to be of value, they must earn the respect and trust of the parties at an early stage of the negotiations and over time through developing a rapport with and gaining the confidence of those who participate in trials before the ALJs. Trial staff must also demonstrate expertise in procedural and substantive matters. This is important for the parties and for the adjudicators. As former Chief Judge Zwerdling observed:

> the hearing examiners' view is that results which are both fair to the parties and consistent with the public interest can be best reached if the staff is subject to the same standards and rules of procedure as the private parties, and if the staff positions are required to be presented in open hearings, where they can be made to stand the test of cross-examination and rebuttal, to compete for approval on the same basis and on the same terms as the private parties.[4]

A year later, in an article for the *Administrative Law Review,* Chief Judge Zwerdling echoed these comments and added:

> the weight given to the staff positions should depend strictly on their merits, and no "brownie points" should be given to such positions simply because they are espoused by the staff.[5]

In 1982, former FERC General Counsel Charles A. Moore further delineated trial staff program goals and expectations in "The New Trial Program at the Federal Energy Regulatory Commission." Trial staff were to advance:

- Development of clear, consistent positions—based on an analysis of the relevant legal and policy precedents,
- Production of well-researched, well-reasoned, and well-articulated pleading—based on legal homework, careful writing and judicious editing,

- Allocation and resources to the trial effort—based on greater emphasis on trial work and the long-range benefits of a strong trial program,
- Development of reasonable settlement positions—based on the range of evidence that could be established at trial,
- Production of a strong litigation effort if a case does not settle—based on management supervision of and support for each trial attorney's work.[6]

Leaders of a trial staff should also be mindful of the observations made in 1973 by former Chief Judge Zwerdling. He acknowledged that trial staff are committed to serving their client, the public interest. However, he emphasized that:

> the problem ... arises from the fact that the staff is not an impersonal machine. It is made up of a cross-section of human beings. This cross-section includes staff people who are extremely able, hard-working and devoted. The cross-section, however, also sometimes demonstrates certain other not unusual characteristics, such as: (1) stubbornness; (2) intellectual laziness; (3) rigidity and narrowness of viewpoint, including a mental block against opening the mind to positions inconsistent with conclusions reached at an earlier stage; (4) in some cases, a mediocre level of ability; (5) a normal human desire to prevail or "win."[7]

Most importantly, for trial staff to be effective, they must be viewed as an unwavering representative of the public interest, with no biases toward the position of any party. Trial staff attorney or expert witness positions should not be based on personal opinions or favoritism. Trial staff must demonstrate that they have "no private axe to grind" and must come across as a voice of reason and moderation. In keeping with these guidelines, when trial staff believe that existing precedent is out of date and in need of FERC reconsideration, they should first present a result based on precedent and then follow up with a view on why the precedent should be reconsidered and how it should be modified. Following this practice enhances the credibility of trial staff's settlement positions and formal positions if settlement is not reached.

The location of the trial staff within an agency is an important consideration, given that outside practitioners might question trial staff's independence if the lines between decision maker and advocate blur. Since the 1930s, trial staff at FERC have been housed in various offices. For many years, trial staff attorneys were located in the Office of General Counsel (OGC) and expert witnesses were located in the technical offices. The same attorneys would also draft orders for cases not in the hearing to which they were assigned. The supervisors of the order-drafting personnel were part of FERC's decisional staff.

In 1982, the OGC appointed a manager and six attorneys to supervise a specific area of FERC's trial practice.[8] In 1984, the supervision of the trial function was transferred to the chief trial counsel. Trial attorneys and expert witnesses continued to come from the divisions responsible for drafting orders and advising the Chair and Commissioners.[9] In 1988, trial attorneys were relocated to a new division within OGC that was dedicated exclusively to trial work.

In 1998, former FERC Chairman James J. Hoecker created the Office of Administrative Litigation (OAL) as part of an overall program designed to streamline FERC activities, improve the quality of its work, and enhance its reputation for fairness and objectivity. OAL consolidated the attorneys and technical staff that participate in hearings before ALJs. The OAL Director reported to the Chairman but was still subject to the separation of functions rule, which bars any informal communication with employees of FERC's decisional process (viz., Commissioners and advisory staff). For the first time, the trial staff were dedicated to cases set for hearing and to the settlement judge process.

Top Sheets

Through the years, FERC's trial staff have demonstrated their value in enhancing settlement prospects in gas and electric utility rate cases. One especially useful tool in doing so is the top sheet. Top sheets reflect trial staff's initial assessment of the issues based on precedent, policy, and facts known at the time of preparation. And although the role played by trial staff is one of advocate, rather than neutral, the top sheet provides an early neutral evaluation of the rate case.

On April 1, 1976, FERC implemented top sheet procedures to aid parties in settling rate cases.[10] The impetus behind this was the belief that top sheet procedures would obviate the need for preparation of detailed testimony and exhibits. It was contemplated that the use of top sheets would shorten the time required to serve trial staff's position on the other parties and might lead to faster settlement of rate cases than if a formal hearing was conducted.

The timing of top sheets preparation is critical because top sheets are circulated prior to staff taking a formal position in the cases via testimony or pleadings. As such, they provide the basis for staff to facilitate settlement discussions prior to commencement of the trial.

Typically, the settlement process seeks to:

- Limit the time, expense and resources that would otherwise require a variety of pleadings, discovery, testimony preparation, cross-examination, initial briefs, reply briefs, initial decision, briefs on exceptions, briefs opposing exceptions, FERC order on the initial decision, requests for rehearing, FERC order on rehearing, and the possibility of filing an appeal with the US Court of Appeals;
- Provide refunds earlier to customers for rates charged in excess of a just and reasonable rate;
- Protect ratepayers from paying no more than a reasonable return on investment;
- Provide regulatory certainty to corporations so that they may make informed short and long-term investments;
- Ensure that terms and conditions of service are fair and nondiscriminatory.

Once completed, the information and analyses encompassed in the top sheets are provided to the parties in the case. Following service of the top sheet, trial staff convene a settlement conference and commence settlement discussions. During the settlement conference, trial staff explain their top sheet and the rationale and precedent underpinning each adjustment made to the pipeline or utility's rate filing. After reviewing staff's adjustments, the intervenors and the regulated entity will usually question trial staff's conclusions and may present counteroffers.

Like settlement documents, top sheets are privileged and confidential. They are not served on decisional authorities or filed with FERC. Top sheets are also not available to non-parties, and they cannot be used in any litigation should settlement discussions prove unsuccessful. The hope for the top sheet process as a settlement tool has been realized; eighty percent of routine cases involving top sheets reach a settlement.

Having looked at dispute systems design in the federal realm through the lens of FERC, we now shift to the development and integration of ADR in state utility commissions.

CHAPTER 8

Exploring ADR in State Regulatory Commissions

Through the lens of three active commissions—the California Public Utilities Commission (CPUC), the New York Public Service Commission (NYPSC), and the Michigan Public Service Commission (MPSC)—we explore varying approaches to and results of dispute systems design efforts for state regulatory agencies. While there are consistencies across the programs (e.g., less formal options for resolving consumer complaints), the processes and programs vary depending on stakeholder or regulatory agency needs and pressing issues.

Consumer Complaints

Each of the three commissions has a well-designed system that provides options for consumers to access information and resolve their concerns or complaints with utility providers. Consumer complaints involve retail residential, commercial, and industrial customers with electric, gas, water, and telecommunications service. All three of the programs described in the following sections start with an informal resolution process. The goal of the informal process is to address issues early and off the record. If the parties are not satisfied with the results of the informal process, they may move to a more formal process.

California Public Utilities Commission

For decades, the CPUC has been committed to options for informally resolving consumer complaints. The CPUC made this a more explicit process in the 1970s. Since then, the CPUC has dedicated staff to a consumer complaint unit. The unit, which has been housed in different parts of the CPUC organization, is now located in the Consumer Affairs Branch (CAB), which is part of the Consumer Protection and Enforcement Division.[1] In addition to helping consumers resolve their complaints, the CAB staff answer questions and assist customers with billing and service matters. In 2018, the CAB received over 26,000 calls and written contacts, with their work resulting in one million dollars in refunds to consumers.[2] The CAB hires employees with at least three years of customer service experience; senior staff train new employees on the CPUC regulations and responsibilities. Committed leadership and dedicated funding and resources have been critical to the development of this robust program.

The consumer complaint process begins with an informal complaint from a consumer. The CAB staff ask the consumer to first contact their utility. If this does not resolve the issue, then CAB staff talk to the consumer about their issues and then contact a designated utility representative. Using facilitation and mediation skills, the CAB staff work with the parties to resolve their differences through this informal process. If the differences are not resolved in favor of the consumer, the consumer may appeal to the next level of CAB/CPUC staff, who will review the complaint and the utility's response and then render a determination. The CAB staff notify the consumer of the determination; if not completely satisfied with the outcome, the consumer may file a formal complaint with the CPUC. Once a consumer complaint is formally filed, an ALJ is assigned to the case. The ALJ will likely inform the parties about the CPUC's formal ADR Program in which ALJs, who serve as neutrals or mediators, assist the parties to resolve their disputes. The CPUC formal ADR Program is discussed later in this chapter.[3]

New York Public Service Commission

The NYPSC Office of Consumer Services (OCS) staff handles consumer complaints and answers questions from consumers.[4] In an April 2015 report, the OCS reported that it handles about 250,000 customer contacts annually and, of those, about 30,000 are forwarded to service providers for investigation and reply.[5]

In 2002, the OCS developed the Quick Resolution System (QRS) to provide timely resolution to those consumers who experience a problem. Under QRS, the consumer must first contact their service provider to seek assistance from the provider. The QRS requires service providers to contact customers with a collection or service issue within two working hours and all other customers by the close of business the following day. The service provider is expected to discuss the matter with the consumer and take the necessary action within fourteen days to resolve their complaint. QRS objectives are to:

- Provide consumers with a satisfactory resolution within the designated time frames,
- Reduce the number of complaints associated with a service provider by allowing them a chance to resolve the matter under the QRS program, and
- Provide OCS staff with additional time and resources to handle more difficult consumer matters that require staff intervention.

If the consumer is not satisfied with the service provider's resolution, they may contact or recontact OCS. At that point, OCS will classify the case under the Standard Resolution System (SRS) and OCS staff will become involved. OCS will submit the complaint to the service provider for investigation and response. The service provider has ten calendar days to respond with a written explanation of the actions it took in response to the QRS complaint and explain why it believes no further action is required. The OCS staff will review the information and work with the parties to resolve their issues. If the parties are unable to reach an agreement, OCS staff will direct the provider to take further action or provide the customer with an explanation of why the provider isn't required to take further action.

If the consumer is not satisfied with the OCS decision, they may request an informal hearing with OCS. The hearing officer is an impartial member of the NYPSC who has not been previously involved in the case. If the consumer and provider are unable to resolve the complaint, then the hearing officer will make a decision and notify the parties. If unsatisfied with the decision rendered by the hearing officer, the consumer can file a formal appeal with NYPSC Commissioners. The appeal must either contend that the hearing officer made an error that affected the decision or provide new evidence that will affect the decision. The NYPSC Commissioners may uphold, change, or reject the decision or return the decision to the hearing officer for review. This system is designed to give the consumer many process options to express their concerns and, hopefully, through these options, resolve their dispute before making a formal appeal.

In a June 2004 report, showing that the QRS objectives were achieved, OCS stated that the number of complaints OCS recorded declined after implementing QRS.[6] OCS further stated that in the first fifteen months of the QRS implementation

90 percent of the customers who contacted OCS before contacting their provider had their cases handled satisfactorily. Additionally, in 2004, the OCS developed a Customer Service Response Index (CSRI) to capture the level of customer service and responsiveness provided by each service provider. OCS collects information on the QRS and SRS complaints and inputs this data into a formula to calculate the CSRI for every utility.[7] Since 2004, the OCS has reported the CSRIs to the NYPSC Commissioners and published them on the NYPSC's website. The April 2015 QRS report states: "The service providers delivering above-average customer service will be commended accordingly. Any service provider whose performance indicators report a weakness will be required to submit a plan outlining the steps it will take to improve its performance."[8] This promotes accountability and provides incentive to respond quickly and effectively.

Michigan Public Service Commission

When consumers have inquiries or complaints, they contact MPSC staff;[9] in 2018, MPSC staff handled over 16,000 inquiries and complaints.[10] When the consumer contacts MPSC with a complaint, MPSC staff will notify the utility, with the expectation that the utility will reach out to the consumer within three days and respond with a report to MPSC within ten days. This conciliation process encourages the parties to talk. If MPSC is satisfied with the utility's response, then MPSC will close the case and send a letter to the consumer notifying them that the case is closed. If the MPSC is not satisfied, it will keep the case open and continue to work with the consumer and the utility until it considers the case closed. Consumers who are unsatisfied with the results may file a formal complaint with the MSPC. The Director of the Customer Assistance Division stated that the staff resolves most disputes.

Nevertheless, though infrequent, some consumers file formal complaints. A formal complaint involves a hearing before an ALJ. ALJs encourage the parties to settle and, if they don't, the ALJ will proceed with a hearing. In a formal telecommunications consumer complaint involving $1,000 or less, the parties are required to attempt to settle or mediate the dispute before going to hearing. In a formal video services consumer complaint involving $5,000 or less, the parties are required to mediate the dispute before going to hearing.

The Customer Assistance Division has a training and policy manual for new employees; in addition, new employees listen to experienced employees during their calls. Other MPSC offices and the Customer Assistance Division exchange information and meet with each other to discuss issues important to each office.

For example, when the MPSC plans to issue an order in a rate case, the appropriate offices meet with the Customer Assistance Division staff the day before the order's release to discuss what will be in the order, preparing the Customer Assistance Division staff with information to answer the calls they may receive once the order is released.

In 2016, the Customer Assistance Division began asking consumers who participated in this process to complete a survey about their satisfaction with the process. Management reviews all the surveys indicating dissatisfaction and uses the results to improve the process. Survey results indicate consumers who aren't satisfied with the outcome don't distinguish between their dissatisfaction with the outcome and their opinion of the process; they say they are unsatisfied with the process when they really meant they were not satisfied with the outcome.

Need-Specific ADR Programs

CPUC ADR Program

ALJs hear the individual consumer cases, as described earlier, and more generic cases affecting many customers, such as a utility filing for a rate increase. Once the case is in the ALJ Division, formal ADR options are available to the parties.[11] The ALJ ADR Program has an interesting history.

Although the CPUC had used ADR prior to 2005, the ADR process was informal and often parties were entrenched in the case before they considered ADR. In 2005, seeing an opportunity to expand the use of ADR, the CPUC ALJ office initiated a study to assess the needs of a formalized CPUC ADR Program to examine opportunities to expand the informal process and to develop implementation plans for an expanded program. The CPUC held focus groups of staff, attorneys, utilities, and nonprofit and advocacy organizations to assess the desirability and characteristics of an expanded ADR Program. The CPUC hired an outside party to facilitate the focus groups and report the results. The ALJs, who would become the ADR neutrals, were not involved in the focus groups. In August 2005, the CPUC adopted Resolution ALJ-185 (Resolution).[12] The Resolution allowed for the ALJs to be facilitators and provide early neutral evaluations. The Resolution stated:

> ADR processes are often preferable to a litigated result because they potentially can produce outcomes that are more responsive to the parties' needs, more consistent with the public interest, avoid the narrow results of litigation . . . encourage more

active participation of all parties . . . save the parties' time and resources, and allow the Commission to direct its decision-making resources to other important proceedings.

In anticipation of the expanded ADR Program, twenty-six ALJs received ADR training, including from the FERC Dispute Resolution Service (DRS) staff, the federal courts, and the California Commission on Judicial Education and Research. The ALJs worked with CPUC staff to integrate the expanded program into existing processes. ALJ management and the Commissioner appointed to the case flagged cases suitable for ADR. If the parties wanted ADR, then the ALJ management evaluated the suitability of ADR for the case, and when appropriate, assigned an ALJ as a neutral to mediate it. The ALJ neutral was never the same ALJ who heard the case. Therefore, ADR continued to be available after the case was assigned to a hearing ALJ. In addition to serving as mediators, the ALJs facilitate discussions and workshops, including those designed to collect input for CPUC policy development and rulemakings.

In 2009, the CPUC ADR Program was evaluated in "The Alternative Dispute Resolution Program and the California Public Utilities Commission: An Update Through Calendar Year 2009" (2009 Report). The 2009 Report stated that since 2005, when the program began, one hundred formal and informal matters incorporated ADR services (most frequently mediation and facilitation and a few early neutral evaluations). In 2009, neutrals handled thirty-four formal and informal matters, a new yearly high, compared to a yearly range of sixteen to twenty-five in prior years. Using settlements or partial settlements and successful facilitation as a measurement, the success rate was 71 percent in 2009 and 69 percent cumulatively since 2005. The 2009 Report further pointed out that: "distilling program success to such statistics, . . . fails to capture other benefits of ADR, which may include less-controversial, better designed, and more durable solutions and sometimes . . . reduced expenditure of time and financial resources." In 2009, the CPUC added a confidential evaluation to its website to make it easier for participants to provide completely anonymous and timely feedback on the ADR Program. Evaluation responses were generally positive and most participants found the formal ADR Program to be fair, to reduce litigation costs, and to shorten the time to resolve the dispute.

To increase ADR use, the 2009 Report suggested an intensified routine focus on reviewing new filings to identify those suitable for ADR and an intensified educational effort. The Chief Judge and the ALJ management team commenced a review to assess all new filings for ADR opportunities. The ADR Coordinator then followed up on the assessments with the ALJ assigned to the case, attended prehearing conferences, and looked for other opportunities to describe the ADR Program. The effort aimed to target filings for mediation, identify filings where mediation could be an effective tool in reducing the scope of the litigated issues, and pinpoint opportunities where facilitated workshops might foster better understanding and streamline the proceeding. If the parties expressed interest, the Chief Judge, at the recommendation of the ADR Coordinator, would assign an ALJ as a mediator or facilitator. The 2009 Report noted education as an ongoing challenge given the turnover of CPUC staff, utility personnel, and practitioners. The ALJ Division met with outside groups to raise ADR awareness and with the CPUC staff to increase awareness and understanding of the ADR Program.

The following are typical steps in the CPUC formal ADR process:

- The ALJ assigned to hear a case will likely discuss ADR with the parties at the first prehearing conference. The parties may then elect to go to ADR. The parties also may request ADR by contacting the assigned ALJ or the ADR Coordinator at any time before or after filing their case.
- After the parties elect ADR, the ADR Coordinator will evaluate the suitability of the case for ADR and will accept or reject the request. If the case is accepted, the ADR Coordinator recommends it for an ALJ neutral assignment.
- Once assigned, the ALJ neutral contacts the parties to discuss the ADR process, confidentiality, and the time and place for the first meeting. The ALJ neutral also distributes a confidentiality agreement to be signed by the parties in advance of the start of the ADR process.
- The ALJ neutral may request the parties provide information in advance of the first session and may require that the parties participating in the process have the authority to commit to a settlement.

The time required to conclude less complex cases ranges from a half day to two full days. More complex cases require more meetings with the neutral and may occur over consecutive days or on a few days each week over several weeks. Once the case settles, the ALJ neutral provides guidance to the parties on how to request CPUC approval or provides other procedural directions, as appropriate.

The program is continually evaluated to identify opportunities for improvement. For example, at the time of this writing, an analysis is being conducted to capture the types of cases settled by each ALJ, with an eye toward matching certain types of cases to certain ALJs in the future. Also the ADR Coordinator is working more closely with the CAB to identify cases suitable for ADR before the parties file a formal complaint and to make the consumer more aware of ADR options. CAB staff is also being included in ADR processes to help deescalate issues. Additionally, there is a continual exploration of enhanced opportunities to promote the ADR Program and to make ADR available before the parties become entrenched in their positions. And ADR is now mandatory in water rate case filings.

In 2017, the ADR Coordinator prepared a second report: "The Alternative Dispute Resolution Program June 2017 Report" (2017 Report). Highlights from the 2017 report are:

- Twenty ALJ trained neutrals are available for ADR.
- Since 2005, the ADR Program provided ADR services in about 250 formal and informal matters, largely resulting in cost-effective settlements.
- Using settlements or partial settlements and successful facilitation as a measurement, the program's cumulative success rate since 2005 is 76 percent, which also includes several of the recent years when annual ADR success rates hovered around 90 percent.
- Adjudicatory proceedings (complaints and investigations) represent on average about half of each year's ADR Program caseload. The other half consists of a few informal matters (disputes resolved without a formal filing), various applications, and rulemakings.
- The case subject matter is varied and includes energy, communications, water, and rail crossing issues.

The 2017 Report further states:

> The Commission's ADR Program often yields outcomes preferable to a litigated result. That is because it has the potential to produce outcomes that are customized to the parties' particular needs or the complexities of public interest considerations, avoid the potentially narrow range of outcomes of litigation that may not adequately address the parties' concerns, encourage more active participation of all parties (regardless of an individual party's size or resources), save the parties' time

and resources, and allow the Commission to direct its decision-making resources to other important proceedings.

In short, the ADR Program has reaped dividends for parties, the public, and the CPUC—a testament to the importance of leadership commitment, flexibility, and continual outreach and evaluation in crafting a process tailored to the unique needs and challenges of the CPUC.

NYPSC and MPSC Telecommunications

The NYPSC and the MPSC developed dispute resolution programs that addressed the needs of the telecommunications industry. Both programs address disputes between businesses.

The NYPSC developed the Expedited Dispute Resolution Process for Disputes Involving Competing Telecommunications Carriers.[13] Historically, the NYPSC used ADR to settle disputes between incumbent common carriers and retail competitors. In November 1999, the NYPSC issued guidelines for an expedited dispute resolution process for operational disputes that were beyond the scope of the parties' interconnection agreements. The process was not designed to be a substitute for the ADR processes in the parties' interconnection agreements. Two resolution processes were available: analysis by appropriate technical staff and, if required, a written advisory decision from the Director of the Office of Telecommunications, or mediation with an NYPSC ALJ serving as the mediator. This process was particularly effective in facilitating disputes when competitive local exchange carriers relied heavily on access to incumbent carriers' facilities and is used less frequently with the emergence of intermodal competition from digital cable networks, wireless networks, and over-the-top providers.

In the late 1990s, the MPSC developed arbitration and mediation rules for disputes involving telecommunications interconnection agreements (telecommunications rules).[14] As mentioned earlier, arbitration is similar to litigation in that the arbitrator (like a judge) renders a decision. With that said, arbitration is an alternative, with parties typically spending less time and money than they would spend in a litigated proceeding. Often these cases are complicated with fifty to seventy-five issues in a single case.

Under the telecommunication rules, arbitration works as follows: The party initiating the arbitration files a petition with the MPSC and serves it on the other party. The petition must include certain dates specified in the rules, an explanation of the issues and positions of the parties, and all relevant information supporting the respective positions. Within twenty-five days of the filing date, the party responding to the petition for arbitration must file a response that includes information on which the party will rely to support its position. A responding party may raise issues not included in the petition. A single arbitrator or a panel can conduct the arbitration.[15] This arbitration is structured, not as a contested proceeding, but as an opportunity to inform the arbitrator or panel of the parties' positions. The disputing parties are the only parties to the arbitration; they do not have the right to conduct discovery. Additionally, any questioning comes from the arbitrator or panel. The arbitrator or panel issues a written decision with the reasons for the decision. The arbitrator or panel has to limit its decision to selecting the position of one party, unless the result would be clearly unreasonable or contrary to the public interest. The parties may file objections to the arbitrator's or panel's decision. Then the MPSC Commissioners issue an order approving, modifying, or rejecting the decision.

Under the telecommunication rules, mediation works as follows. For mediation required by statute and for informal dispute resolution, the MPSC may designate an MPSC staff member, an ALJ, or an outside person to serve as the mediator. The process is evaluative. After working with the parties, the mediator will issue a recommended settlement and send it, under seal, to the parties in the mediation and to the Executive Secretary of the MPSC. The parties file, under seal, their acceptance or rejection of the settlement with the Executive Secretary of MPSC. The Administrative Law Manager reviews the filings and advises the MPSC and the parties if a hearing is required.[16] If the case proceeds to hearing, the recommended settlement and the parties' responses remain sealed until the MPSC issues a final order in the case.

The MPSC orders accepting the outcome of the arbitration or mediation are subject to federal court proceedings. The goal of the arbitration and mediation process is to produce a sustainable outcome. In one instance, a dispute between incumbent carriers and new entrants that had been in the courts for seven years was remanded to the MPSC and settled through mediation.

MPSC—Uniform Video Services Local Franchise Act

The Uniform Video Services Local Franchise Act (UVSLF Act) gives the MPSC some regulatory authority over video service providers, such as cable companies and telecommunications companies providing video services that have franchise agreements with local governments to serve their area.[17] The UVSLF Act required the video service providers and the MPSC to implement dispute resolution procedures. Each video service provider was required to establish a dispute resolution process for disputes with its customers and to notify its customers at least annually of the process. The process must be posted on the provider's website. Before a customer can file a complaint with the MPSC, they must first attempt to resolve the dispute using the provider's dispute resolution process. When the MPSC receives a customer complaint, MPSC staff will attempt to resolve the dispute through mediation. If the dispute is not resolved, the customer may file a formal complaint with the MPSC.[18]

For provider and franchising entity disputes or disputes between providers, the UVSLF provisions provide for informal and formal resolution steps. The provider or franchising entity must first file a notice of the dispute with the MPSC and serve it on the other party. The MSPC staff will conduct an informal mediation to resolve the dispute. If the dispute is not resolved, any party to the dispute may file a formal complaint with the MPSC. When a party files a formal complaint, the complaining party must state the section(s) of the UVSLF Act or parts of the franchise agreement that it believes the other party violated, include all material supporting its allegations, and state the relief it requests. For sixty days after a formal complaint is filed, the parties attempt alternative means of resolving the complaint. Within ten days after the complaint is filed, if the parties cannot agree on the alternative means, the MPSC will order mediation. The process is evaluative. Within sixty days after the MPSC orders the mediation, the mediator is required to issue a recommended settlement. Within seven days after that, each party files with the MPSC a written acceptance or rejection of the recommended settlement. If the parties accept the recommended settlement, it becomes the final order. If a party rejects the recommended settlement, then the complaint proceeds to a contested case hearing and the recommended settlement is kept under seal until the MSPC Commissioners issue a final order. A party rejecting the recommended settlement pays the opposing party's actual costs of proceeding to a contested case hearing, including reasonable, non-excessive attorney fees, unless the MPSC

Commissioners' final order is more favorable to the rejecting party than the recommended settlement. A final order is considered more favorable if it differs by 10 percent or more from the recommended settlement in favor of the rejecting party. The MPSC UVSLF program provides parties with multiple avenues to resolve their disputes. Since the inception of the program, most of the cases have settled.

Value of Distributed Energy Resources

The NYPSC also incorporates dispute resolution tools in its work. One example of this is the facilitation effort to address all aspects of Value of Distributed Energy Resources (VDER).[19] After a conference in May 2017 to elicit stakeholder input, the NYPSC issued an order in the VDER case to form three working groups, responding to stakeholder input at the conference and to the need for transparency and balancing of stakeholder interests. Each group focuses on a specific topic, holds regular meetings, distributes information through shared emails, develops its own work plan and schedule, and includes active participants and observers. NYPSC staff spearheads the facilitation of this process to compile information, solicits input from all stakeholders, and develops recommendations to send to the NYPSC Commissioners.

NYPSC Interconnection Policy Working Group

NYPSC staff is also facilitating the Interconnection Policy Working Group (IPWG). An NYPSC staff member leading the IPWG initiative and a counterpart from the New York State Energy Research and Development Authority joined together to cofacilitate the IPWG. Prior to forming the IPWG, they talked with stakeholders to better understand the systemic issues. With information gathered regarding the extent of the issues, they recommended formation of the IPWG.

At NYSPC's staff request, the NYPSC Secretary issued a letter on June 17, 2016, to parties in the VDER case, announcing the formation of the IPWG to address nontechnical issues related to distributed generation (DG) interconnections.[20] The staff would convene and facilitate the IPWG efforts and would specifically address interconnection queue management. The IPWG makeup would reflect the variety of stakeholders impacted by interconnection polices. Affected parties were asked to express their interest in participating in the IPWG to the NYPSC staff and provide a brief description of their interests. The interconnections got on track and generation projects started moving. The IPWG stakeholders developed a plan for interconnection queue management, and some of the parties filed it with the NYPSC; the plan went into effect in January 2017. The cofacilitators continue to work with the IPWG to assist the stakeholders in resolving other issues and to develop more formal procedures for IPWG deliberations.

MPSC: Implementing New Energy Legislation

MPSC staff incorporated facilitation and consensus-building tools to implement Public Acts 341 and 342 signed into law by Michigan Governor Rick Snyder on December 21, 2016.[21] Public Laws 341 and 342 updated Michigan's energy laws relating to utility rate cases, electric choice, Certificate of Necessity, electric capacity resource adequacy, integrated resource planning, renewable energy, energy waste reduction, distributed generation, and on-bill financing program implementation. The laws went into effect April 20, 2017, and, in some cases, impacted existing programs in 2017.

MPSC staff, under the leadership of the Director of the Strategic Operations Division, developed a consensus-building effort to ensure implementing the new legislation was open and transparent. The MSPC staff looked at the requirements of Public Laws 341 and 342 and designed a process to effectively address each issue, including detailed steps and timelines. They convened, led, and facilitated discussions of eighteen different stakeholder groups, each responsible for a different topic. The topics the stakeholder groups addressed included rate case and Certificate of Necessity filings, integrated resource planning processes, resource adequacy, electric choice, renewable energy, distributed generation, energy waste reduction, and demand response. Often the stakeholder groups developed consensus recommendations for the MPSC staff to send to the MPSC Commissioners. The recommendations informed the Commissioners' deliberations and decision-making. We highlight two process examples—rates filings and the integrated resource planning processes.

One of the rate case filings groups addressed the new requirement that lowered the time for the MPSC to process rate cases from twelve months to ten months, with the goal of providing more information to the parties up front rather than in discovery. MPSC staff facilitated a collaborative process, through which interested parties expressed their ideas and concerns. MPSC staff then developed a draft document for the parties to review and discuss. The parties discussed the document and provided written comments; the MPSC staff considered all the comments and on June 9, 2017, sent a final proposal to the MPSC Commissioners. In July 2017, the

MPSC Commissioners issued an order adopting standard rate case filing forms and instructions.

The MPSC staff used facilitation tools with the integrated resource planning group. Integrated utilities must file an Integrated Resource Plan (IRP), and the new legislation required the MPSC to produce a model for individual utilities to use to develop their IRP and to allow the public to comment on the model before it was final. The MPSC staff developed an informal pre-collaborative and formal collaborative process to address this requirement. The steps in the informal pre-collaborative process were: an initial stakeholder meeting, full group and interest-area subgroup meetings, preparation and presentation of a strawman proposal by the MPSC staff along with the Michigan Agency for Energy and the Michigan Department of Environmental Quality, stakeholder comment on the strawman proposal, and an MPSC staff report including the revised strawman proposal and a summary of the comments. The MPSC staff facilitated the meetings and this process.

The next step was for the MPSC staff to initiate the formal collaborative process. The MPSC issued an order to do so, and the MPSC staff posted the latest strawman proposal in the docket. The MPSC staff then held public hearings around the state and took questions and verbal comments. Stakeholders also had the opportunity to provide written comments. The MPSC staff prepared a report, detailing the comments and providing a revised model. The MPSC staff posted the report and recommended model in the docket. Finally, the MPSC Commissioners, using the report, deliberated and issued an order. The successful pre-collaborative and collaborative processes demonstrate the MPSC's commitment to party participation in a timely fashion, allowing interested parties adequate opportunities to provide their input and views.

Summary

These programs exemplify how exploration and implementation of ADR tools may enhance both the process to address contested issues and the outcome achieved. And although each of the programs is unique—designed to respond to the distinct challenges of the respective state agency—each program exemplifies the importance of leadership, funding, flexibility, outreach, training, and evaluation in achieving a program that is responsive, well-supported, and sustainable.

CONCLUSION

Throughout this book, we shed light upon the opportunities for ADR in the federal and state regulatory arenas. And although we spent considerable time showcasing the model programs at FERC and at state utility commissions in California, Michigan, and New York, our overarching message is not to replicate these programs but rather to highlight the importance of the *process* of developing, implementing, and integrating an ADR Program into an organization. One size does not fit all. Although the robust and far-reaching use of ADR at FERC is instructive, the approach that FERC took to develop and integrate ADR is more instructive. Similarly, although the expansion of skills development and ADR use in the CPUC has translated into impressive statistics, the continual analysis and evaluation that have informed this expansion are even more impressive.

The Voices of Value model outlined previously provides a starting point for the development, expansion, and integration of ADR Programs at federal and state regulatory agencies, regulated entities, and private sector companies. This model does not, however, provide an endpoint at which agencies or organizations can check a box to indicate that the design is complete. The model is meant to be iterative, continually informed by the effectiveness of and response to current ADR use. These components of the model are captured in the themes of *opportunity, empowerment,* and *sustainability,* which apply equally as well to regulatory agencies, regulated entities, and private sector companies.

As demonstrated through the examples in this book, there are multiple *opportunities* to employ ADR throughout agencies and private sector companies. FERC's integrated approach to ADR, offering multiple entry points, exemplifies that there is rarely one answer to the question of how an agency or organization can better manage disputes. Mediation might prove an effective tool for some cases; however, solely employing this process could lead to missed opportunities for other ADR applications. Inherent to FERC's effectiveness was the recognition that there is more than one opportunity for ADR. Correspondingly, there is more than one ADR approach or process that will meet all agency and organizational needs around managing disputes.

The second component, *empowerment,* undergirds the effectiveness of ADR Program development and integration. Empowerment of agency and company leaders, ADR Program personnel and neutrals, agency and company staff, and other parties fosters an environment to recognize and seize upon the opportunities of ADR throughout an agency or organization. The empowerment of leaders is the starting point because, as underscored previously, leadership is essential to develop a successful and effective ADR Program. Leaders empower others with a mandate to seize opportunities of ADR, a budget to implement ADR Programs, and support to ensure that the ADR initiatives are meaningfully integrated. But first, leaders must be empowered with knowledge of the value of ADR. This knowledge may come from a variety of sources: training for leaders, in which they experience the transformative potential of ADR; evaluations that aim to quantify the value of ADR efforts; feedback from parties about their experiences with ADR; dialogue with offices about the results of incorporating ADR practices into their work; and networking with other agencies and companies that have vibrant ADR Programs, as well as corresponding data to share about the program impact.

Leadership endorsement is a critical starting point because it empowers ADR Program personnel with the mantle to introduce and/or expand ADR. To do so effectively, ADR Program personnel must have a comprehensive understanding of ADR tools and applications. The understanding may come through training and/ or information sharing, which happens extensively in the federal ADR community and through entities such as the American Bar Association Section of Dispute Resolution. The understanding may also come from practitioner groups, who might be able to offer insight or outside resources.

ADR Program personnel must also be empowered with the freedom to take risks in program implementation. Doing so gives program personnel the space to capitalize on opportunities. It also involves regular, built-in reflection on the program. Just as there is more than one opportunity for ADR at an agency or organization, there is more than one opportunity to create or tweak a program. Along the same lines, neutrals must be empowered with the mandate to practice ADR at the agency or organization. Going back to a theme early in the book: ADR processes are meant to complement, rather than replace, traditional processes. There are plenty of disputes to go around. Fostering a culture that values the different process options for resolving disputes—from informal to formal—sets the stage for success. ADR neutrals must also be empowered with skills development opportunities to effectively meet the challenges of the cases in which they are involved. Just as lawyers or accountants need to take continuing legal education courses to stay apprised of developments in their respective fields, ADR neutrals should be supported in their efforts to stay apprised of theoretical and practical developments and lessons learned in ADR.

Agency staff, regulated entity staff, and private-sector company staff must also be empowered with knowledge. Staff must understand ADR process options and the relationship between those options and the work of the larger agency or organization. There is sufficient work to go around. ADR process options are designed to complement that work and provide yet another avenue to resolve conflict. Staff must be empowered with knowledge of how they might employ ADR options within their respective offices or individual work. This can be accomplished through training in areas such as negotiation, facilitation, and communication. Even when staff are not sitting in a mediator's chair, they may find themselves facilitating a public meeting or navigating a difficult conversation with a party to a dispute; ADR skills will better equip them to do this.

Finally, parties need to be empowered with knowledge and understanding of the dispute resolution tools and options that are available throughout the agency or organization. This requires comprehensive outreach. Parties must know how to access the hotlines and helplines that are designed to answer their questions and provide a quick resolution to their disputes. Parties must understand the more structured dispute resolution processes (e.g., mediation) offered by an agency or organization and how to initiate these processes. Parties must also understand what the varied dispute resolution processes encompass. They must know, for example, that mediation is generally voluntary and that they will not relinquish their rights by opting to participate. Parties must be provided with tools to effectively prepare for these processes, such as handouts and electronic resources on what to expect and how to engage in a dispute resolution process.

The third component, *sustainability,* may be the most important consideration in ADR Program development and expansion. Although the initial enthusiasm and support for ADR implementation is important to initiate the culture shift, the ADR experiment will fail without built-in mechanisms to ensure program sustainability.

As long-time dispute resolution practitioners, we have worked with agencies and organizations to launch and/or expand ADR Programs. There is considerable momentum at first; it is up to ADR champions to carry on that momentum.

Several things are critical to a sustainable program. Dedicated *funding and resources* lend institutional credibility and legitimacy to an ADR Program, which can insulate it from organizational shifts and changing priorities. ADR Programs with dedicated funding and resources are more viable than are those without. There may be a commitment at the program level for ADR; however, without committed funding, ADR initiatives can easily become an afterthought.

As demonstrated through the federal program at FERC and the state programs in California, Michigan, and New York, successful and meaningful ADR requires much more than a verbal commitment to ADR. Meaningful ADR requires a comprehensive analysis of opportunities and potential entry points. Once identified, subsequent steps must be mapped to seize these opportunities, from designating program staff, to *training,* to promoting *outreach.* A concerted effort is necessary to plant the building blocks for ADR integration into an agency or organization. That requires funding and resources.

Tracking and evaluation are essential to the success and sustainability of an ADR Program. Tracking can help identify trends and potential areas for expansion. Evaluation can help to identify what works well and what might be tweaked. This is important in the formative stages of ADR Program development. Tracking and evaluation are even more important as a program evolves. Organizational changes and turnover can impact agency or organization priorities, and ADR Programs may be vulnerable. Statistics to demonstrate the impact of ADR are essential to justify ADR's value. Having the data to demonstrate how many concerns are addressed and conflicts resolved using ADR tools is powerful.

Mapping trends over the years may highlight the need to maintain or increase funding. Support for agency or organization-wide training in practical ADR skills, such as communication and facilitation, may be bolstered by quantifying how many people inside and outside the agency or organization participate in training programs and by following up with training attendees to capture the impact. Quantifying how much time or money is saved through mediating a case is difficult, in part because that requires conjecture into the "what if?" But there are comparators, such as the number of staff hours to litigate a case. There are also comparators for those entities engaged in the cases, including how the life of a mediated case compares with the average life of a litigated case.

It is also powerful to capture the impact of a dispute resolution process on the relationship between landowners and a pipeline company or different electric utilities. This qualitative data can provide a baseline to understand trends and pinpoint impact. If, for example, regular litigation adversaries engage in mediation and subsequently spend more time communicating and less time litigating, then the qualitative benefits of mediation have a far-reaching impact.

In short, tracking and evaluation must be integrated into an ADR Program from the outset because times change and leaders change. Hard numbers regarding the number of cases settled and the number of trainings offered internally and externally is powerful. Equally powerful are data demonstrating the value of ADR. Collectively, these numbers form the basis for the argument about why support of ADR makes sense, funding should continue, and resources should be dedicated.

Throughout this book, we highlighted success stories and lessons learned through the promotion and application of ADR. The lessons learned and the successes realized do not signal that the work is done. In the federal and state realms, the programs of FERC and California, Michigan, and New York are model programs because the agencies continue to evolve to meet the needs of their stakeholders as well as their own needs. Just as the success endures, the work endures as well. There continue to be untapped opportunities in federal and state regulatory agencies and private sector companies that, in some cases, have just scratched the surface of ADR potential. We hope the programs here provide both guidance and inspiration to continue the journey to fully realize the potential of ADR. It will be worth the effort!

NOTES

Introduction

1. From Administrative Conference of the U.S., *Sourcebook: Federal Agency Use of Alternative Means of Dispute Resolution,* (Office of the Chairman, 1987). archive.org/stream/gov.acus.1987.adr/sourcebook1987unse_djvu.txt. For the quoted language from the ABA's Commission on Law and the Economy 1979 report, which describes the shortcomings of the administrative processes, see Charles Pou Jr., "Federal Agency Use of 'ADR': The Experience to Date," in *Federal Regulation: Roads to Reform* (Washington, DC: ABA Commission on Law and the Economy, 1979), 102,

2. Warren E. Burger, "Agenda for 2000 A.D.: A Need for Systematic Anticipation," *The Pound Conference: Perspectives on Justice in the Future,* ed. A. Leo Levin and Russell R. Wheeler (St. Paul, MN: West Publishing, 1979), 32.

3. Jerome T. Barrett, with Joseph P. Barrett, "A History of ADR: The Story of a Political, Cultural, and Social Movement," traces ADR to traditional societies such as the Bushmen of the Kalahari, the Yoruba of Nigeria, and the Kpelle of Central Liberia (San Francisco: Jossey Bass, 2004), 2–5.

4. The statutory mission of the Administrative Conference is (1) to study all aspects of federal agencies' procedures; (2) to identify and analyze the causes of administrative inefficiency, delay, and unfairness; and (3) to recommend to Congress or to the executive and independent agencies means of improving the quality of administrative justice. 5 U.S.C. §§ 591–596.

5. Administrative Conference of the United States, "Recommendation 86-3: Agencies' Use of Alternative Means of Dispute Resolution" (June 20, 1986). https://www.acus.gov/recommendation/agencies-use-alternative-means-dispute-resolution.

6. See Marshall J. Breger, "Chairman's Foreword," *Sourcebook: Federal Agency Use of Alternative Means of Dispute Resolution* (Office of the Chairman, 1987), iv, archive.org/

stream/gov.acus.1987.adr/sourcebook1987unse_djvu.txt.

7. Ibid.

8. Administrative Dispute Resolution Act, Pub. L. No. 552, 104 Stat. 2736.

9. 5 U.S.C. § 581(3), *redesignated,* 5 U.S.C. § 571(3), *see* S. Rep. No. 101–543, at 1 (1990); H.R. Rep. No. 101–543, at 2–3 (1990). Congressional findings in support of the 1990 ADR Act were:

   - Administrative procedure . . . is intended to offer a prompt, expert, and inexpensive means of resolving disputes as an alternative to litigation in the federal courts.
   - Administrative proceedings have become increasingly formal, costly, and lengthy, resulting in unnecessary expenditures of time and diminished likelihood of achieving consensual resolution of disputes.
   - Alternative means of dispute resolution have been used in the private sector for years and, in appropriate circumstances, have yielded faster, less expensive, and less contentious decisions.
   - Such alternative means can lead to more creative, efficient, and sensible outcomes.
   - The availability of a wide range of dispute resolution procedures will enhance the operation of the government and better serve the public.

10. The 1990 ADR Act also stated that ADR should *not* be considered when
    - A definitive or authoritative resolution of the issue is required;
    - The matter involves questions about government policy;
    - Maintaining established policies is of particular importance;
    - The matter affects individuals or entities besides the parties;
    - A full public record is important; or
    - The agency must maintain continuing jurisdiction over the matter.

11. Administrative Dispute Resolution Act, Pub. L. No. 552, 104 Stat. 2736, § 2; S. Rep. No. 101–543, at 1 (1990); H.R. Rep. No. 101–513, at 11–12 (1990).

12. Administrative Dispute Resolution Act of 1996, 5 U.S.C. §§ 571–584 (1994 & Supp IV 1998).

13. Order No. 32, 44 Fed. Reg. 34,936 (1979), FERC Stats. & Regs., Reg. Preambles 1977–81 ¶ 30,061.

14. Pub. L. No. 102–486, 106 Stat. 2776 (1992).

15. Notice of Proposed Rulemaking, 69 FERC. ¶ 61,180 (1994).

16. Federal Energy Regulatory Commission, FY 2016 Congressional Performance Budget Request 2 (2015).

17. Ari Peskoe, *Alternative Dispute Resolution at Public Utility Commissions* (Cambridge, MA: Harvard Law School, 2017), 11. Also see WAC § 480-7-700(3)(a).

18. Peskoe, *Alternative Dispute Resolution at Public Utility Commissions,* 11. Also see Resolution ALJ-185, "Expanding the Opportunities for and Use of Alternative Dispute Resolution Processes at the Public Utilities Commission," August 25, 2005.

Chapter 1. Coming Together of the Regulatory Context and ADR Tools

1. Charles F. Phillips Jr., *The Regulation of Public Utilities, Theory and Practice* (Public Utility Reports, 1984), 6, as quoted in Martin Shapiro, *The Supreme Court and Administrative Agencies* (New York: Free Press, 1968), 260–61.

2. Jonathan Raab, *Using Consensus Building to Improve Utility Regulation* (Washington, DC: American Council for an Energy-Efficient Economy, 1994), 8.

3. Werner Troesken, "Regime Change and Corruption: A History of Public Utility Regulation," in *National Bureau of Economic Research, Corruption and Reform: Lessons From America's History* (Chicago: University of Chicago Press, 2006), http//www.nber.org/chapter/c9986.

4. Catherine M. Sharkey, "The Administrative State and The Common Law: Regulary Substitutes or Complements?," *Emory Law Journal* 65 (2016): 1711. See also, *Gellhorn and BYSE's Administrative Law, Cases and Comments,* 9th ed. (Westbury, NY: Foundation Press, 1995), 15–16.

5. Pub. L. 79-404, 60 Stat. 237.

6. 5 U.S.C. § 554(c) (1982)(1). Emphasis added.

7. Charles Pou Jr., "Federal Agency Use of 'ADR' to Date," in *Sourcebook: Federal Agency Use of Alternative Means of Dispute Resolution* (Office of the Chairman, 1987), 102, footnote 3, http://www.archive.org/details/sourcebook1987unse.

8. Ibid.

9. S. Capobiano et al., *Conflict Dynamics Profile* (St. Petersburg, FL: Eckerd College Leadership Development Institute, 1999), 1.

10. C. Runde and T. Flanagan, *Becoming a Conflict Competent Leader: How You and Your Organization Can Manage Conflict Effectively* (San Francisco: Jossey-Bass, 2013), 46.

11. William L. Ury, Jeanne M. Brett, and Stephen B. Goldberg, *Getting Disputes Resolved: Designing Systems to Cut the Costs of Conflict* (San Francisco: Jossey-Bass, 1988), 3.

12. Leigh Thompson, *The Mind and Heart of the Negotiator,* 5th ed. (Pearson, 2014), 2.

13. Stephen Frenkel, "Power Differentials in Negotiation: Don't Let 'Em Push You Around," *Harvard Negotiation Law Review,* October 21, 2009, https://www.hnlr.org/2009/10/addressing-power-differentials-in-negotiation-dont-let-em-push-you-around/.

14. Zena Zumeta, "Styles of Mediation: Facilitative, Evaluative, and Transformative Mediation," www.mediate.com/articles/zumeta.cfm.

15. Ibid.

16. Cathy Constantino and Christina Sickles Merchant, *Designing Conflict Management Systems* (San Francisco: Jossey-Bass, 1996), 124.

Chapter 2. Designing a Sustainable Dispute Resolution System

1. Cathy Constantino and Christina Sickles Merchant, *Designing Conflict Management Systems: A Guide to Creating Productive and Healthy Organizations* (San Francisco: Jossey-Bass, 1996), xiii.

2. Ibid., 49.

3. Ibid., 106. Constantino and Merchant's question for systems design within an organization are broadly applicable, including in the federal and state regulatory realm.

4. Constantino and Sickles Merchant, *Designing Conflict Management Systems,* 169.

5. Stephen F. Gates, "Ten Essential Elements of an Effective Dispute Resolution Program," *Pepperdine Dispute Resolution Law Journal* 8, no. 3 (2008). https://digitalcommons. pepperdine.edu/drlj/vol8/iss3/5.

6. Ibid.

7. Jonathan Raab, *Using Consensus Building to Improve Utility Regulation* (Washington, DC: American Council for an Energy-Efficient Economy, 1994), 48.

8. In "Alternative Dispute Resolution: Why It Doesn't Work and Why It Does," Carver and Vondra highlight companies where top management, deciding that "winning at all costs was too expensive," evaluated "lawyers, contract managers, and paralegals not merely on lawsuits won or lost but on disputes avoided, costs saved, and the crafting of solutions that preserve[d] or even enhance[d] existing relationships." Todd B. Carver and Albert A. Vondra, "Alternative Dispute Resolution: Why It Doesn't Work and Why It Does," *Harvard Business Review* 72, no. 3 (May–June 1994): 120–130, https://hbr.org/1994/05/alternative-dispute-resolution-why-it-doesnt-work-and-why-it-does.

9. Gates, "Ten Essential Elements an Effective Dispute Resolution Program."

10. A recent interview of Larry Susskind, the founder of the Consensus Building Institute (CBI) at MIT, touches upon this issue. According to Susskind, neutrals should be literate in the substance of the issues being negotiated; they need not be technical experts, but they better be "quick studies" who are curious about the science behind the issues. "Fireside Q&A with Professor Larry Suskind," interview by Natalie Watkins, *EDR Blog,* University of Utah S. J. Quinney College of Law, April 25, 2016, http://www.law.utah.edu/fireside-q-a-with-professor-larry-susskind/.

11. Constantino and Sickles Merchant, *Designing Conflict Management Systems,* 144.

12. Ibid.

13. Ibid., 135.
14. Ibid., 145.
15. Ibid., 143.
16. Ibid.
17. Raab, *Using Consensus Building to Improve Utility Regulation,* 42.
18. Ibid., 43–44.
19. Ibid.
20. Constantino and Sickles Merchant, *Designing Conflict Management Systems,* 158.
21. Ibid., 153.

Chapter 3. Ensuring Dispute Resolution System Integrity

1. "About the MPSC," Michigan Public Service Commission, 2019, https://www.michigan.gov/mpsc/0,4639,7-159-16400—,00.html
2. "Inquiries and Complaints," Michigan Public Service Commission, 2019, https://www.michigan.gov/mpsc/0,4639,7-159-16368_16415—,00.html
3. MISO FERC Electric Tariff at .https://cdn.misoenergy.org/Tariff%20-%20As%20Filed%20Version72596.pdf ; specifically Attachment HH at https://cdn.misoenergy.org/Attachment%20HH109885.pdf; also MISO Business Practices Manual BMP 23 at https://www.misoenergy.org/legal/business-practice-manuals/.
4. For the complete version of the Standards, see "Model Standards of Conduct for Mediators," September 2005, https://www.americanbar.org/content/dam/aba/migrated/dispute/documents/model_standards_conduct_april2007.authcheckdam.pdf.
5. Administrative Dispute Resolution Act, Pub. L. No. 552, 104 Stat. 2736.
6. 5 U.S.C. § 574.
7. Alternative Dispute Resolution, Notice of Proposed Rulemaking, Docket No. RM91-12-000, 69 FERC ¶ 61.180 (1994) and 5 U.S.C. § 554(d).
8. See 18 C.F.R. § 385.606.
9. See 18 C.F.R. §§ 385.604 and 605.
10. Notice of Proposed Rulemaking, Docket No. RM91-12-000 (Nov. 18, 1994), FERC Stats. & Regs., Proposed Regs. 1988–1998, ¶ 32,510, at 32,926 (1994).
11. 18 C.F.R. § 385.606(c).
12. 18 C.F.R. §§ 385.606(a) and (b).
13. 18 C.F.R. § 385.606(d)(1).
14. 18 C.F.R. § 385.606(e).
15. Stephen R. Melton, "Separation of Functions at the FERC: Does the Reorganization of the Office of General Counsel Mean What It Says?," *Energy Law Journal* 5, no. 2 (1984): 349.

16. See 18 C.F.R. 385 § 2202 (2016); Order 718, 73 FR 62886, Oct. 22, 2008. This Rule, along with the APA's provision, is found at 5 U.S.C. § 554(d). This rule conforms to a long-standing jurisprudence principle that an advocate should not judge his own case. See Bonham's Case, 8 Co. 114A, 118 (1610) and 3 Davis, Administrative Law Treatise 2d, 430–431 (1980).

17. Statement of Administrative Policy on Separation of Functions, 101 FERC ¶ 61,340, at ¶ 32 (2002).

18. Administrative Dispute Resolution Act, Pub. L. No. 552, 104 Stat. 2736.

Chapter 4. Examining the Application and Integration of ADR at the Federal Energy Regulatory Commission

1. These responsibilities stem from various laws, such as the Federal Power Act, Public Utility Regulatory Policies Act, Natural Gas Act, and Interstate Commerce Act. More recently, as part of the Energy Policy Act of 2005, Congress gave FERC additional responsibility to protect the reliability and cybersecurity of the bulk electric power system through the establishment and enforcement of mandatory standards, as well as additional authority to enforce FERC regulatory requirements through the imposition of civil penalties and other means. FERC meets these statutory requirements by establishing rules and policy that will result in just, reasonable, and not unduly discriminatory or preferential rates, terms, and conditions of jurisdictional service; increasing compliance with FERC rules; detecting and deterring market manipulation; fostering economic and environmental benefits for the nation through approval of natural gas and hydropower projects; and minimizing risks to the public associated with FERC jurisdictional energy infrastructure.

2. Order 602, 64 FR 17097, Apr. 8, 1999, as amended by Order 647, 69 FR 32438, June 10, 2004; Order 734, 75 FR 21505, Apr. 26, 2010; Order 821, 81 FR 5379, Feb. 2, 2016.

3. 18 C.F.R. § 1b.1.

4. 18 C.F.R § 1b.21(e).

5. See "Enforcement Hotline," FERC, https://www.ferc.gov/enforcement/staff-guid/enforce-hot.asp.

6. 18 C.F.R. § 1b.22.

7. "Alternative Dispute Resolution," FERC, https://www.ferc.gov/legal/adr.asp.

8. 18 C.F.R. § 385.605.

9. 18 C.F.R. § 385.604(d).

10. 18 C.F.R. § 385.604(e) requires the following:

- A proposal to use alternative means of dispute resolution must be in writing and include the following:
  (1) A general identification of the issues in controversy intended to be resolved by the proposed alternative dispute resolution method,
  (2) A description of the alternative dispute resolution method(s) to be used,
  (3) Signatures of all participants or other evidence indicating the consent of all participants, and
  (4) A certificate of service pursuant to Rule 2010(h).

11. 18 C.F.R. § 385.604(f).

12. 56 FERC ¶ 61,437 (1991).

13. 56 FERC ¶ 61,437 at 62,559 (1991).

14. 18 C.F.R. § 385.605(c).

15. 18 C.F.R. § 385.605(d).

16. 18 C.F.R. § 385.605(d).

17. 18 C.F.R. § 385.605(e)

18. FERC cases discussing arbitration include *Kansas Gas and Electric Co.,* 28 FERC ¶ 61,112 (1984); *Texas-New Mexico Power Co. v. El Paso Electric Co.,* 30 FERC ¶ 61,242 (1985); *Transcontinental Gas Pipe Line Corp.,* Order Approving Settlement, as Modified and Issuing Certificates, 55 FERC ¶ 61,446 (1991), *reh'g denied,* 57 FERC ¶ 61,345 (1991), *aff'd Elizabethtown Gas Company v. FERC,* 10 F.3d 866 (1993); *American Municipal Power-Ohio, Inc. v. Dayton Power and Light Co. 56 FERC* ¶ 61,437 (1991); Madison Gas and Electric Co., 56 FERC ¶ 61.447 (1998); *N. Carolina E. Mun. Power Agency v. Carolina Power & Light Co.,* 45 FERC ¶ 61,487 (1998); *Duquesne Light Co.,* 83 FERC ¶ 61,042 (1998); *Cities of Anaheim, Azusa, Banning, Colton and Riverside, California and the City of Vernon, California v. California Independent System Operator Commission,* 101 FERC ¶ 61,235 (2002); *New York Indep. Sys. Operator, Inc.* 105 FE.R.C. ¶ 61,249 (2003), *reh'g granted in part and denied in part on other grounds,* 109 FERC ¶ 61,163 (2004); *Lavand & Lodge, LLC v. ISO New England Inc.,* 126 FERC ¶ 63,005 (2009); *Twin Valley Hydroelectric,* 148 FERC ¶ 61,127 (2014).

19. See Complaint Procedures, Order No. 602, FERC Stats & Regs. ¶31,071 at 30,756, 30,768, *order on reh'g,* Order No. 602-A, 88 FERC ¶ 61,114, *order on reh'g,* Order No. 602-B, 88 FERC ¶ 61, 294 (1999).

20. Settlements in Hydropower Licensing Proceedings under Part I of the Federal Power Act, *Policy Statement on Hydropower Licensing Settlements,* 116 FERC ¶ 61,270 (2006).

21. See16 U.S.C. § 803(a)(1)(2000).

22. 116 FERC ¶ 61,270.

23. See 18 C.F.R. § 4.38 for original license and 18 C.F.R. §16.8 for relicenses.

24. 18 C.F.R. § 4.34(i)(2)(ii).

25. 18 C.F.R. Part 5.

26. See Order No. 2002-A, *Hydroelectric Licensing under the Federal Power Act,* 106 FERC ¶ 61,037 (2004).

27. For a copy of this report, see https://www.ferc.gov/industries/hydropower/gen-info/ licensing/ilp/eff-eva/ideas.pdf.

28. Order No. 608, Collaborative Procedures for Energy Facility Applications, Order No. 608, 64 FR 51209 (Sept. 22, 1999); FERC Stats. & Regs., Regulations Preambles ¶ 31,080 (Sept. 15, 1999).

29. 18 C.F.R. § 250.16(b)(1).

30. Pub. L. No. 102–486, 106 Stat. 2776 (1992).

31. Revisions to Oil Pipeline Regulations pursuant to the Energy Policy Act of 1992, Order No. 561, 58 Fed. Reg. 58783 (Nov. 4, 1993), III FERC Stats. & Regs. 30,985 (1993), *order on reh'g and clarification,* Order No. 561-A, 59 Fed. Reg. 40243 (Aug. 8, 1994), III FERC Stats. & Regs. 31,000 (1994).

32. C.F.R. § 385.343.5. See also Order 578, 60 FR 19505, Apr. 19, 1995.

33. See Promoting Wholesale Competition Through Open Access Non-Discriminatory Transmission Services by Public Utilities; Recovery of Stranded Costs by Public Utilities and Transmitting Utilities, Order No. 888, 61 Fed. Reg. 21540 (1996), FERC Stats. and Regs., Regulations Preambles January 1991–June 1996 ¶ 31,036, at 31,730–32 (1996), *order on reh'g,* Order No. 888-A, 62 Fed. Reg. 12274 (1997), FERC Stats. and Regs., Regs. Preambles July 1996–Dec. 2000 ¶ 31,048, at 30,278–79 (1997), *order on reh'g,* Order No. 888-B, 81 FERC ¶ 61.248 (1997), *order on reh'g,* Order No. 888-C, 82 FERC ¶ 61,046 (1998).

34. Order No. 888, FERC Stats. & Regs. ¶ 31,036 at 31,732.

35. See Regulations for Filing Applications for Permits to Site Interstate Electric Transmission Facilities, Order Denying Rehearing, 119 FERC ¶ 61,154 at 36.

36. Order No. 578, FERC Stats. & Regs. ¶ 31,018.

37. 18 C.F.R. § 385.604.

38. 18 C.F.R § 385.604(a)(2).

39. In Public Utility District No. 2 of Grant County, 89 FERC ¶ 61,177 (1999), a party requested that the Commission order Grant County to enter into mediation under Rule 604. The Commission denied the request, noting Grant County's opposition to the request and Rule 604's requirement that participants concur in a mediation request.

40. 18 C.F.R. § 385.604.

41. 18 C.F.R. § 385.604(a)(3).

42. 18 C.F.R. § 385.604(a)(2)(i)–(vi).

43. See Complaint Procedures, Order No. 602, FERC Stats & Regs. ¶ 31,071 at 30,756, 30,768, *order on reh'g,* Order No. 602-A, 88 FERC ¶ 61,114, *order on reh'g,* Order No. 602-B, 88 FERC ¶ 61, 294 (1999).

44. See 18 C.F.R. § 385.206(b)(9).

45. The names of the parties have been intentionally deleted and replaced with "the complainants" or "the parties."

46. 86 FERC ¶ 61,324 (1999).

Chapter 5. Appreciating the Role of an Independent Dispute Resolution Staff

1. FERC, "Commission Plans Major Changes to Keep Pace With Regulated Industries," news release, June 11, 1998, p. 2.

2. Ibid.; see accompanying fact sheet, p. 2.

3. Initially, the DRS was located in FERC's Office of the General Counsel. In 2005, the DRS was relocated to FERC's Office of Administrative Litigation. In 2013, the DRS was relocated to the Office of Administrative Law Judges. In 2019, the DRS returned to the Office of the General Counsel. See FERC, "FERC's Dispute Resolution Service to Join Office Admin. Law Judges," press release, June 14, 2013, http://www.ferc.gov/media/news-releases/2013/2013–2/06–14–13.asp#.Ufcer-BU7f4.

Chapter 6. Resolving Cases with the FERC Settlement Judge Process

1. Michael Asimow, "The Administrative Judiciary: ALJs in Historical Perspective," *Journal of the National Association Law Judiciary* 19, no. 2 (1999): 27.

2. See Northern Pennsylvania Power Company & Metropolitan Edison Company, 1 F.P.C. 350, September 1936.

3. See 2 F.P.C. 633, 634 (1939).

4. 5 U.S.C. § 554(c) (1982) and Pub. L. 79-404, 60 Stat. 237.

5. John W. Macy Jr., "The APA and the Hearing Examiner: Products of a Viable Political Society," *Federal Bar Journal* 27 (1967): 351, 353.

6. Butz v. Economou, 438 US 478, 513-14 (1978).

7. 5 U.S.C. § 554(c) (1982) (emphasis added).

8. The paper is sourced from the personal files of Richard Miles.

9. FERC Rules of Practice and Procedure, Order No. 90, 45 Fed. Reg., 45,902 (1980), FERC. Stat. and Regs., Reg. Preambles 1977–81, ¶ 30,169.

10. See 47 Fed. Reg. 19104, 19,021 (1982).

11. 18 C.F.R. § 385.603.

12. 18 C.F.R. § 385.603(c).

13. 18 C.F.R. § 385.603(d).
14. 18 C.F.R. § 385.603(e).
15. 18 C.F.R. § 385.603(f).
16. 18 C.F.R. § 385.603(g).
17. 18 C.F.R. § 385.602(g).
18. 18 C.F.R § 385.602(f).
19. 18 C.F.R. § 383.602(f)(4).
20. 18 C.F.R. § 385.602(g).
21. 18 C.F.R. § 385.602(h).
22. 18 C.F.R. §§ 385.602(e)(1), (e)(2).

Chapter 7. Looking at the Role of Independent Trial Staff in the Settlement Process

1. Joseph Zwerdling, "The Role and Functions of Federal Hearing Examiners," *The Annals of the American Academy of Political and Social Science,* vol. 400 (March 1972): 30.
2. Staff have participated in FPC hearings as early as 1935. See Pigeon River Lumber Company, 1 F.P.C. 206, May 1935, Southern Industries & Utilities, Inc., 1 F.P.C. 219, June 1935. Staff's participation also included the presentation of evidence. See Safe Harbor Water Power Corporation, 1 F.P.C. 230, 234, June 1932.
3. Joseph Zwerdling, "Reflections on the Role of an Administrative Law Judge," *Administrative Law Review* 25, no. 1 (1973): 17.
4. Zwerdling, "The Role and Functions of Federal Hearing Examiners," 30.
5. Zwerdling, "Reflections on the Role of an Administrative Law Judge," 17.
6. Charles A. Moore, "The New Trial Program at The Federal Energy Regulatory Commission," *Energy Law Journal* 3, no. 2 (1980): 338.
7. Zwerdling, "Reflections on the Role of an Administrative Law Judge," 17–18.
8. Moore, "The New Trial Program at The Federal Energy Regulatory Commission," 338.
9. For a fuller discussion of this topic as viewed in 1985, see Stephen B. Melton's "Separation of Functions at the FERC: Does the Reorganization of the Office of General Counsel Mean What It Says?" *Energy Law Journal* 5, no. 2 (1984).
10. See Order No. 157, "Top Sheet Procedures in Natural Gas Pipeline and Public Utility Rate Cases" (April 1, 1976), 41 Fed. Reg. 15.090 (1976).

Chapter 8. Exploring ADR in State Regulatory Commissions

1. See "File a Complaint," California Public Utilities Commission (CPUC), https://www.cpuc.ca.gov/complaints/; and "Consumer Affairs Branch—Utility Portal," CPUC, https://

consumers.cpuc.ca.gov/CABUtilityComplaint.aspx.

2. See CPUC, "2018 Annual Report," pp 30–31, https://www.cpuc.ca.gov/uploadedFiles/ CPUC_Public_Website/Content/About_Us/Annual_Reports/CPUC%20Annual%20 Report%20-%20Draft%201-31-19%20-%20page%20view%20-%20red%20sz.pdf.

3. The CPUC formal ADR Program allows parties to enter the ALJ Division's ADR Program before filing a formal complaint or before the assigned ALJ discusses ADR with the parties.

4. 16 NYCRR, Subchapter B. Procedures and Requirements Concerning Consumer Protections, Part 12. Consumer Complaint Procedures, http://www3.dps.ny.gov/N/ nycrr16.nsf/Parts/35B3B58DB01B0CE485256FC7004CFBA7?OpenDocument; and New York State Department of Public Service, "Filing Your Complaint with PSC," http://www3.dps.ny.gov/W/PSCWeb.nsf/ All/755C4F39A58C924C85257B2F0067FCA5?OpenDocument.

5. New York State Department of Public Service, Office of Consumer Services, Quick Resolution System, under Complaint Handling Guide for Service Providers, April 2015, Ver. 2.5, p. 3, http://www3.dps.ny.gov/W/PSCWeb.nsf/All/ FA05AA0D1F13FED085257687006F3A81?OpenDocument.

6. For report, see Customer Service Response Index (CSRI), Office of Consumer Services, June 2004, Ver. 2.2, pp. 2–3, http://www3.dps.ny.gov/W/PSCWeb. nsf/96f0fec0b45a3c6485257688006a701a/fa05aa0d1f13fed085257687006f3a81/$FILE/ CSRI_Details_V2.2.pdf. For data, see CSRI, https://data.ny.gov/Energy-Environment/ Utility-Company-Customer-Service-Response-Index-CS/w3b5-8aqf/data.

7. CSRI, Office of Consumer Services, "Measuring the Responsiveness of Service Providers in New York State," June 2004, Ver. 2.2, pp 3–7, http://www3.dps.ny.gov/W/PSCWeb. nsf/96f0fec0b45a3c6485257688006a701a/fa05aa0d1f13fed085257687006f3a81/$FILE/ CSRI_Details_V2.2.pdf.

8. New York State, Department of Public Service, Office of Consumer Services, Quick Resolution System, under Complaint Handling Guide for Service Providers, April 2015, Ver. 2.5. p. 10, http://www3.dps.ny.gov/W/PSCWeb.nsf/All/ FA05AA0D1F13FED085257687006F3A81?OpenDocument.

9. See "Inquiries and Complaints," Michigan Public Service Commission, https://www. michigan.gov/mpsc/0,4639,7-159-16368_16415—,00.html.

10. Michigan Public Service Commission, "2018 Annual Report," March 4, 2019, p 9, https:// www.michigan.gov/documents/mpsc/MPSC_2018_Annual_Report_647843_7.pdf.

11. The CPUC formal ADR Program allows parties to enter the ALJ Division's ADR Program before filing a formal complaint or before the assigned ALJ discusses ADR with the parties.

12. Resolution ALJ-185, August 25, 2005, "Expanding the Opportunities for and Use of Alternative Dispute Resolution Processes at the Public Utilities Commission."

13. NYPSC, Case 99-C-1529, November 18, 1999.

14. See order in MPSC, Case No. U-11134, July 16, 1996 and rules in "MPSC Procedures for Telecommunications Arbitrations and Mediations." These rules govern practice and procedure before the MPSC in the arbitration proceedings required by section 252(b) of the Federal Telecommunications Act of 1996, 47 U.S.C. 252(b), and in the mediation proceedings conducted under MCL 484.2203a, MCL 484.3106, MCL 484.3107, or MCL 484.3310(5)(b)(i) and (6)(b).

15. See MPSC Procedures for Telecommunications Arbitrations and Mediations, part 2, R 484.704 Designation of Arbitration Panel or Arbitrator, for a detailed description of the arbitrator or arbitration panel.

16. The ALJs who hear MPSC cases are not part of the MPSC. They are part of the Michigan Administrative Hearings System's Public Service Commission Division, which is managed by the Administrative Law Manager.

17. See Uniform Video Services Local Franchise Act, Act 480 of 2006, as amended by Act 4 of 2009 and Act 191 of 2009, compiled by Michigan Public Service Commission staff, April 21, 2010.

18. If the dispute involves an amount of $5,000.00 or less, the MPSC appoints a mediator who makes recommendations for resolution within thirty days from the date of their appointment. Within ten days of the date of the mediator's recommendations, any party to the complaint may request the MPSC to initiate a contested case hearing.

19. NYPSC, 15-E-0751, In the Matter of the Value of Distributed Energy Resources, June 22, 2017.

20. Letter from NYPSC Secretary to parties in Case 15-E-0751, June 17, 2016.

21. Act No. 341, Public Acts of 2016, approved by the Governor, December 21, 2016, effective April 20, 2017. Public Act No. 342, Public Acts of 2016, approved by the Governor, December 21, 2016, effective April 20, 2017.